Doing Gender in Heavy Metal

Doing Gender in Heavy Metal

Perceptions on Women in a Hypermasculine Subculture

Anna S. Rogers
Mathieu Deflem

ANTHEM PRESS

Anthem Press
An imprint of Wimbledon Publishing Company
www.anthempress.com

This edition first published in UK and USA 2022
by ANTHEM PRESS
75–76 Blackfriars Road, London SE1 8HA, UK
or PO Box 9779, London SW19 7ZG, UK
and
244 Madison Ave #116, New York, NY 10016, USA

British Library Cataloguing-in-Publication Data
A catalogue record for this book is available from the British Library.

Library of Congress Control Number: 2021946520

ISBN-13: 978-1-83998-133-3 (Hbk)
ISBN-10: 1-83998-133-4 (Hbk)
ISBN-13: 978-1-83998-136-4 (Pbk)
ISBN-10: 1-83998-136-9 (Pbk)

This title is also available as an e-book.

CONTENTS

PREFACE AND ACKNOWLEDGMENTS

In this work, we present a sociological investigation of perceptions concerning the contemporary presence and reception of women in the heavy metal community. Framed in feminist perspectives of "doing gender," this study is based on semi-structured interviews, which for comparative purposes include both men and women who self-identify as fans of heavy metal, in order to assess some of the dynamics and relevance of gender in this traditionally hypermasculine sphere of popular culture. This examination is specifically developed within the framework of the perspective of "doing gender" and relies on an original set of interview data to address specified research questions. What do metalheads themselves think about the manner in which metal women "do gender" when there are (still) relatively few, though undeniably more than before, of them around? What do heavy metal fans themselves see as the opportunities and the obstacles of the process of women claiming their place in the heavy metal (sub)culture? And, how do observed changes of the increasing presence of women in heavy metal lead the way to foster greater equality with respect to gender in this world of rock music. To address these questions, we rely on a unique data set of original interviews and, in the development and discussion of relevant themes, also develop a serious engagement with the existing relevant literature on heavy metal, popular culture, and gender.

The publication of this work as a book that is relatively brief but, we hope, also insightful, rather than in the form of either a journal article or a lengthier monograph, is fitting given the scope of our investigations. The findings of our work rely on semi-structured interviews with a relatively small sample of 20 respondents. This study therefore cannot be oriented at generalization, but is meant to illustratively show the value of our sociological perspective on gender in one area of popular culture. Our approach is most critically aimed at an in-depth qualitative strategy to empirically uncover meaning and identity of self and others in a relatively unique and surely fascinating subculture of popular music. Given these objectives, it would be difficult, if not outright impossible, to write up the results of our work in any meaningful way in a

PREFACE AND ACKNOWLEDGMENTS

journal article or book chapter. Yet, although relatively limited in scope and precise in its focus, our study is oriented at unraveling the perceptions of heavy metal fans concerning the evolving status of the woman metalhead. To convey these subjective but real ideas concerning self and others appropriately, we adopt a narrative approach that, by definition, uses a lot of words, especially as they are articulated by the respondents, to provide proper meaning and nuance. In this sense, publisher Anthem Press presented itself as an ideal opportunity, for us as authors and, hopefully, for the readers as well.

The format of this work and its focus on an aspect of popular culture, we further hope, may enable this book to reach an audience that is both broad, including even some of the very subjects of our study, but also sufficiently specialized and of interest to relevant academic audiences of scholars and students, especially in the areas of gender and (popular) culture. While primarily conceived as a study in the sociology of gender, this book of course also seeks to make a contribution to the scholarly study of popular culture, music, and heavy metal, areas of research that have acquired considerable popularity and to which field both authors of this book have also contributed from their respective viewpoints.

The theme of gender has increasingly been addressed in scholarship on popular culture, including heavy metal, on which subject matter a new field of so-called metal music studies has developed. Yet, while not conceived from within this area but instead framed in the sociology of gender, we do engage with the findings from all pertinent scholarly contributions, no matter their more or less developed and diverging intellectual foundations. Our elaborate engagement with other studies should prevent any misunderstanding of our scholarship as coming from outside the field. Instead, by offering a sociological analysis of gender in the world of heavy metal, we seek to develop a scholarly contribution to, rather than in, the study of music and popular culture. Our approach as scholars to study selected aspects of heavy metal culture in a detached way is all the more appropriate and called for as we are also, as popular music participants, fans of various kinds of heavy metal. The sociological orientation of our work on gender also generally fits the Anthem Press focus on books devoted to our discipline.

This book grew out of graduate work in sociology that was originally developed by the first author under the supervision of the second author. The first author has primarily developed an expertise in the areas of the sociology of gender and popular culture. She conducted all the interviews reported in this book, developed the theoretical perspective, and conducted all analyses of interviews in terms of the research questions she had formulated as well. The second author mostly contributed to finalizing the writing of the book and the integration and presentation of the theoretical and empirical materials within a usefully broad context of relevant findings and perspectives from the literature. He has for several years also been involved in sociological work on popular culture (and shares an interest in deviance and social control with the first author). Given this division of labor, this book should also reveal that both authors have over the years developed a strongly collaborative intellectual partnership. Although pandemic concerns combined with other difficulties to delay the finalization of this work, we were also able to put the extended time to good use to rethink, revise, and strengthen our research and ideas, thereby making this book greatly different from, and hopefully much stronger than, its rather rudimentary original form (Rogers 2015).

Because of our focus on gender, a brief note is in order on some of the terminology adopted in this book. Adopting current social science conventions, we avoid use of the terms male(s) and female(s) except to explicitly denote references to biology or body and/or when these words are used not as concepts but as everyday words by the participants themselves in the heavy metal community, including the respondents of the interviews in our study. Otherwise, we use the terms man/men and woman/women, both as nouns and adjectives, to refer to the cultural construct of gender as the central focus of our investigations.

Preparing and writing this book, we benefited greatly from conversations with some of our nearest mentors and colleagues, especially Brent Simpson, David Melamed, Lynn Weber, and Andrea Henderson-Platt. We thank our dear friend Derek Silva for his sage advice that encouraged us to write this book. Without his support, this work would simply not exist. We also benefited from organizers and audiences at meetings of the American Sociological Association and the Southern Sociological Society, where we presented research on related aspects of popular culture and gender. We are grateful for the support we received from the University of South Carolina, our institutional home at the time the research for this book was conducted. We thank the editors and anonymous reviewers of Anthem Press for their very helpful comments and suggestions that greatly improved this work. We owe especially warm thanks to editor Megan Grieving whose professionalism in overseeing the finalization of this book was matched only by her kindness and generosity. And, of course, we thank the awesome metalheads who agreed to be interviewed for this book.

Anna acknowledges the Bilinski Educational Foundation for offering her a Russell J. and Dorothy S. Bilinski Fellowship for academic year 2018–19, during which time she conducted research toward the writing of this book. She also thanks her great colleagues and awesome students at the University of Georgia where she has since found a welcome home for work. She thanks her brilliant partner Evan Pressman for his love and support, and her sweet

baby bat cat Gremlin for always being by her side during the writing process. She also thanks her brother Matthew for being her lifelong best friend.
Most of all, she expresses her loving gratitude to her mother, Angela Rogers,
for teaching her the value of education, and to her father, Brian Rogers, for
raising her in a home where music was valued.

Mathieu acknowledges the College of Arts and Sciences at the University of
South Carolina for research funding used in support of this project. Mathieu
is also very grateful for Naoko Yoshimura, whom he is thrilled to call *tsuma*.

May we all live to see the dawn.

Chapter 1

GENDER AND POPULAR CULTURE: THE CASE OF HEAVY METAL

She bears a fierceness that you'll underestimate
Don't disrespect her or you she'll devastate
Her essence takes its toll
You're losing all control
She is a metal woman

3 Inches of Blood, "Metal Woman" (*Long Live
Heavy Metal* 2012)

Presenting a sociological study of perceptions on women in the subculture of heavy metal music on the basis of interviews with self-identified fans of the genre, this study is aimed at accurately and usefully describing and portraying what members of the metal community themselves think and feel in their own terms. Rather than examining the (objective) structures of the dynamics and stratification of gender in the heavy metal culture, we develop an interpretive model of various aspects of (subjective) identity of self and (intersubjective) understanding of others in the heavy metal community, with a special focus on questions of gender. Such a perspective oriented at hermeneutic understanding, laying bare subjective meaning, can count on a long and proud tradition in the social sciences, stretching back to the very foundations of the discipline, most notably the work of Max Weber (1949), and enjoying continued popularity and recognition until today. Critically, we will also show that such interpretive work can only be sociologically relevant if it is contextualized within an appropriate theoretical framework (Habermas 1970). As this study will reveal, this methodology sets a sociological investigation often apart from other work that is not disciplinarily guided.

It will be more than useful to bring out, from the start, what this book can and cannot do. This work is not conceived of, nor meant to be, a study in the relatively young field that is nowadays referred to as "metal music studies," "metal scholarship," and "heavy metal studies" (Brown 2011; Gardenour Walter et al. 2016; Spracklen et al. 2011). Of course, we do hope our work can offer relevant insights and would not wish to deny that this variably labeled area of study does not also contain sociological and otherwise disciplinary work, or that it would not have produced interesting studies. In fact, as we will show throughout this book, we have learned much from the relevant literature on heavy metal to situate our own investigations (Chapter 3) and with which we will also engage in terms of the implications for the study of central questions of gender, feminism, and popular culture (Chapter 8).

While research from other fields has been inspirational, especially in terms of relevant empirical findings, this book is primarily and distinctly conceived as a contribution in the sociology of gender that is situated in a realm of popular music. As such, we respond to the growing interest in the study of pop culture among scholars in sociology and gender studies. Gender scholars have by now indeed usefully examined an array of popular culture themes, such as the portrayal of violence against women (Ramon et al. 2021), representations of family (Åström 2015) and other gender roles (Murnen et al. 2016; Rogers 2019), sexual orientation (Lovelock 2019), and the usefulness of such studies for teaching purposes (Genz 2012). Yet, at the same time as sociology can learn from popular culture and its study, so too should pop culture scholars and other practitioners of related areas, such as music and heavy metal, in turn see what they can learn from sociological work. Otherwise, it would be more than a little ironic would an effort such as this book not be welcomed by scholars working in fields that claim not only interdisciplinarity but multidisciplinarity as well. Such irony would be all the worse if it were to affect a junior and a senior scholar of different genders who for several years now have been working fruitfully in tandem.

This book is therefore not to be understood as a study of heavy metal but as a sociological analysis of issues of gender that are revealed in the world of heavy metal. This critical distinction particularly informs why and how we have framed the questions of our research. Sociological research, we argue, must define itself primarily by the questions that are asked on the basis of theory rather than the questions that are presented on the basis of empirical work, let alone the findings presented therein. Of course, because of the sociological orientation and scholarly grounding of our work and its focus on issues of gender in the heavy metal community, we also seek to contribute insights relevant to the existing scholarship on heavy metal, a field of study that we will accordingly engage with throughout this book. Besides its sociological orientation, the appeal of the theme of gender in popular culture toward a broad audience, not just to the metal and music crowd, and its in-depth treatment and discussion should, we hope, also contribute to this book's reception across multiple audiences.

In this opening chapter, we explain and justify our central research focus on the theme of gender in the context of the development of feminist perspectives in the social sciences and, therein, in relation to the issues and questions it poses in the culture of heavy metal music. As our investigations are conceived as an effort in the sociology of gender that is applied to the world of heavy metal, it will be useful to clarify the theoretical basis of this book, its central theme, and the reasons why the heavy metal subculture forms such an interesting arena in which to study pertinent sociological questions of gender. Because the collection and analysis of our data on perceptions concerning women in heavy metal are theoretically grounded, our study cannot answer the otherwise interesting empirical matter of how many women are present in various forms of heavy metal, a statistical matter that is no doubt difficult to estimate. Instead, we examine what gender-related changes and conditions mean at the level of participants' lived experiences.

Heavy Metal and Women

Arguably more so than any other kind of rock 'n' roll, none of the many genres of this form of popular music and its associated culture are thought to be more traditionally masculine and unashamedly manly in its attitude and image than heavy metal is (Christe 2003; Gaines 1998; Recours et al. 2009; Walser 1993; Weinstein 2000). To be sure, other forms of popular music also exhibit distinct gender dynamics, which can be both profound and problematic, especially for women (Trier-Bieniek 2013; Whiteley 2000). Yet, while rock music in general has historically been dominated by men and has largely been marked by conventional masculinity (Cohen 1997, 2001), heavy metal might be claimed to exude these characteristics even more so. Distorted guitars, loud, screaming, and growling vocals, and crashing drums exude the primal screams that are culturally most commonly associated with manhood, maleness, and masculinity, on the part of the performers as well as, indeed, the vast majority of the audience. If there traditionally was a place for women in heavy metal, it was as passive objects of desire and lust, as prey of the chase subservient to (heterosexual) men's needs and wants.

But today, as a wise man once sang, the times they are a-changin', for in recent years women have increasingly moved into the heavy metal community, as performers and devotees alike, to establish by intent or effect the potentials, if not the realizations, of a more gender-egalitarian structure and culture. As a telling indicator of the broad cultural acceptance of gender as an increasingly relevant issue in heavy metal, the current Wikipedia page on "Heavy

Metal Music" devotes an entire section (out of a total of four) to "Women in heavy metal," with its sole subsection dealing with "Sexism." Whether such concerns are empirically justified is a matter of research, but it is striking to note that issues of women and heavy metal have moved centerstage in today's collective consciousness. Thus, gender is understood as relevant, even from within popular culture, because it is seen as an important social and cultural force, especially when equity in gender matters is assumed not to have been achieved. Previewing some of the findings from the literature, scholars studying gender in heavy metal concur (even though exact numbers are unknown) that women have numerically moved more into the metal community, both as fans and as performers (see Chapter 2). However, the implications of this process of heavy metal's (relative degree of) feminization are not nearly as clear, not to the members of the metal subculture itself nor, as we will show, to the community of scholars.

As the study findings will reveal, the participants in our research describe the heavy metal subculture as (still) overrepresented and dominated by men while also arguing that women have increasingly moved (quantitatively) more and more into the metal community in (qualitatively) more diverse and often less traditional ways. The respondents in our interviews generally describe the subculture as changing in a positive direction for women and for the metal community. Women fans of heavy metal, the findings of our research will further show, can especially earn respect from their fellow metalheads through the aggressive act of (hypermasculine) moshing, though they sometimes (yet increasingly more rarely) also engage in a process of defensive othering when they express opinions about, and explicitly distance themselves from, other women fans who engage in (hyperfeminine) flashing.

However, the stated ideas and ideals of a community's members cannot be taken at face value. Thus, the central themes that are revealed in the interviews of our study (see Chapters 5, 6, and 7) are to be taken not as necessarily objectively valid statements but as subjectively held representations of select participants of the heavy metal community itself. Furthermore, precisely because of the undeniable advances that have been made by women in heavy metal, it would be foolish to disregard the lasting influences of heavy metal's lingering past and long-standing traditions. The heavy metal community until today can and must still be described as dominated by men, at least in numbers, but arguably also as hypermasculine in many of its forms and dimensions. Still, it is also clear that things are not as they once were. Changes in gender across many an area of modern culture have affected the many worlds of popular music as well, a development that because of pop culture's popularity alone cannot be trivialized. From the viewpoint of the sociology of gender, therefore, heavy metal is not a mere curiosity in contemporary popular music culture, but instead forms a unique experiment in the field in which to study important gender-related questions of change and resistance, of belonging and separation, and of evolving feminism with respect to both its progress and its setbacks.

Rather than exploring all the many layers and dimensions of the intrinsically complex questions of gender in heavy metal, this study focuses on subjective fan perceptions concerning the woman question in heavy metal. This approach harmonizes with the notion that the heavy metal community can be described as a subculture, that is, as a relatively specific culture that is situated within a broader whole and characterized by its own, distinctive values and behaviors. Employing the concept of subculture to heavy metal does not mean that its community of devotees and musicians is necessarily oppressed by, but instead clearly differentiated from and generally valued less than, a larger cultural sphere from which it distinguishes itself and from which, in turn, it is distinguished by others (Brown 2003; Fine and Kleinman 1979; Gracyk 2016). The subcultural status of heavy metal is relative, as the music and its community have at times also waded into the mainstream but, conversely, also remained removed from full public recognition. Not surprisingly, the subcultural degree of heavy metal has been found to be especially pronounced in highly traditional societies that lack a liberal culture (LeVine 2008; Torreiro 2020; Wong 2011). Moreover, the extent to which the communities of heavy metal (or metal, two terms we use interchangeably) can be described as more or less subcultural will also vary across the musical form's many subgenres that are more or less conventional or, conversely, extreme with respect to music, conduct, and beliefs (see Chapter 7). With these qualifications concerning degree and variation in mind, the concept of subculture can remain fruitful, as the analysis in this book will show.

Based on interviews with an equal number of men and women who identify as fans of heavy metal, the subjectivist approach of our inquiries to examine insiders' opinions is, to be sure, only one element of a much broader problematic begging for systematic research. Yet, we believe our small study can make a valuable contribution precisely by being grounded in empirical data retrieved through semi-structured interviews and does not remain swamped in speculation or conjecture. Our study offers a model to examine the role of women in heavy metal and the metalhead identity and culture that should stimulate interesting and well-grounded questions for further study, precisely because it is based on concrete findings from a relatively delineated but empirically based endeavor that is theoretically framed. Additionally, both the sociology of gender and the sociology of popular culture offer exciting contemporary areas of research—at the intersection of which our book is positioned—that can also contribute to show its value for teaching (Guberman 2020).

The Question of Gender

In the context of this book, we cannot nor need to present an elaborate history of heavy metal as a genre of music and the culture that is associated therewith. Suffice it to say that heavy metal originated in rock 'n' roll from the late 1960s onwards and especially evolved during the 1970s with a focus on increasing levels of guitar-driven loudness and aggressiveness. The music and the culture have in varying degrees been studied by a variety of scholars, as we will discuss in Chapter 3, wherein questions of gender in heavy metal have also been explored. In fact, as will be obvious from the many citations to relevant works in this book and our thorough discussion of the literature, research on women metalheads has expanded considerably over the years, no doubt in some significant part in response to the growing presence of women in heavy metal. However, while ours is obviously not the first study to take on questions of gender and the status of women in the world of heavy metal, it would not be useful to our understanding of gender in music cultures to describe the current scholarship of women in heavy metal as a saturated field of research. The mere fact that similar research has already been done before cannot mean that we (and others) could no longer contribute to such scholarship. It would be absurd to claim that prior work would exhaust an area of study, although we must also show, as we hope to do throughout this work, the value and validity of our research in its own terms. Were we to restrict our research efforts to filling in so-called gaps in the literature narrowly understood on the basis of empirical findings, every topic of inquiry would deserve only a few original studies and we would overlook the fact that science is a process, not an event. Yet, merely offering facts and empirical data on women in metal today also would also not be enough to justify this book. Instead, what our work seeks to add to current scholarship is to address important sociological questions rooted in relevant feminist perspectives to address some of the gender dynamics in the heavy metal subculture by means of interviews with fans of this musical genre and its culture.

The framework of this book is rooted in feminist theories of gender difference and their relevance for the sociology of popular culture. We specifically rely on theories of the threefold themes of othering (including gender performativity), objectification, and doing gender to explore gender issues in the contemporary heavy metal subculture. Our study focuses on the heavy metal community from the point of view of its members' experiences related to gender on the basis of research that shows that homosocial environments consisting of men, involving strong nonromantic social bonds among them, lead to a culture of hegemonic masculinity and attitudes that are disrespectful of, and at times outright hostile against, women, even to the point of engaging in violence (Bird 1996; Miller 1998). From the viewpoint of our sociological approach, we therefore ask how the traditional homosocial world of men in heavy metal has responded to the increasing presence of women among their midst.

In order to uncover the experiences of members of the heavy metal subculture, we report the findings of semi-structured interviews of a total of 20 men and women fans of heavy metal. Men and women are included in this study for comparative reasons to bring out the views of one gender category (men) that is traditionally and commonly thought to be dominant in the world of heavy metal in comparison to the other category (women) that is said to have gained more and more inroads. Our focus on self-identified men and women fans of heavy metal does not imply any argument against research on nonbinary and transgender persons (Gregory 2013). Instead, we rely on the categories men and women to better bring out the role of women in heavy metal, which other research can complement, and provide nuance to, by exploring additional complexities.

While a history of the sociology of gender is beyond the scope of our study, it is useful to note that sociological and related social science perspectives concerning gender and, especially, the status of women in social life are presently in full swing after a much belated start. The relatively recent development of a veritable sociology of gender is remarkable, among other reasons, because feminist scholars have produced scholarly work since at least the late 1800s and the beginning of the women's rights movement. Initially most centrally concerned with women's suffrage, the post–Second World War period witnessed a surge in interest in women's place and role in society. One of the key pieces of literature that led to this second wave of feminism was Simone de Beauvoir's *The Second Sex* (1952). This groundbreaking and classic piece of work focused on women as "the Other" in society. The othering of women, de Beauvoir argued, is impactful in contributing to shape women's subjectivity and accounts for their relative lack of power. While de Beauvoir's book is clearly more of a philosophical nature, it has heavily influenced feminist scholarship and theorizing in sociology and other social sciences. Specifically, it helped shape sociological theories of gender difference and the concepts of sexual objectification and doing gender.

It is this theoretical framework of doing gender that guides the empirical research in this book. Following a brief exposition of de Beauvoir's (1952) classic work on the concept of othering and its impact on the theorizing of feminist scholar Judith Butler (1990, 2004) concerning gender performativity, we will discuss empirical evidence from available research to show that women in groups numerically and otherwise dominated by men "do" their gender and in the process can be objectified and treated as the Other. At the same time, some women may avoid this othering by "not doing" or "undoing" their gender as expected by the dominant cultural order and instead exhibit "masculine" behaviors, thus making it harder for men to treat them as the Other. These theoretical ideas are in this book relied upon to examine how women are perceived, and accordingly treated, with regard to their aspired and realized place in heavy metal. It is important to uncover these internal attitudes within the heavy metal community to understand the cultural environment that creates relevant gender dynamics.

The Homosociality of Heavy Metal

Historically throughout human history, men and women have been confined to separate, respectively public and private, social spheres. Women were traditionally in charge of running the household, while men went out and worked. Today, that situation has changed, although how drastically remains to be seen. For while women have increasingly entered the public sphere in a multitude of ways, they are still not always treated equally or with all due deserved respect, despite the great strides that have been made in recent decades. On the part of men, at the same time, there has also been a rise in the number of stay-at-home dads. Although this percentage is still relatively low, the number of fathers staying home to the care for their children has risen over the past few decades (Kramer et al. 2015).

As a result of such gender-relevant societal changes, fewer places exist today where a true homosocial environment of men and a (hyper)masculine culture can flourish. Although they surely still exist, such as in sports, college culture, gaming communities, certain specialized fandoms related to movies, and other pop culture forms (see Chapter 3), they are generally not as widespread or dominant as before. Homosocial environments denote communities where members of same-gender groups interact in a nonromantic way. Homosocial environments composed of men are known for their hegemonic masculinity that promotes sexism and heterosexism (Lipman-Blumen 1976). They create a hierarchy where men dominate women and where sex and gender differences are used as justifications for gender inequalities. Homosocial environments can include members of the opposite gender, but only as a minority presence, with all due possible inequalities resulting from this structural condition. An environment of outright misogyny can even lead to circumstances where harassment, sexual assault, and violence against women can occur as a result of aggression, sexism, and hypermasculine attitudes.

Certain conditions of homosociality have received quite a bit of public (and scholarly) attention. The popular and commercially lucrative world of professional sports, for instance, is known to lead to at times extreme outbursts of aggression against women. Examples include the handling of some high-profile domestic violence cases involving athletes in the National Football League, which have been reported to have been handled poorly by professional sports organizations, possibly because they occurred in a homosocial environment that justified a dominance of men over women (Doerer 2018). Receiving as yet less attention, though not unheard of, are similar such problematic consequences in the world of rock and metal. Many examples could be mentioned. In the collective memory of American music culture perhaps receiving most attention in the past decades was the physical and sexual violence that was reported against women during a performance of nu metal band Limp Bizkit at, of all places, the Woodstock festival in 1999 (Vanhorn 1999). Other instances of acts of violence at heavy metal shows involved men molesting women who were crowd-surfing (Curry 2017; Hooton 2014), events that tend to get more attention when performers have to berate their own fans when they engage in such actions (Rosenblatt 2017). As more incidents of sexual harassment and sexual assault at metal and other rock shows (as well as in the heavy metal industry) have in recent years been reported, the issue has become recognized as a sufficiently prevalent problem that women have begun organizing efforts to raise public awareness (Kelly 2018; Pasbani 2020). The most spectacular incidents of heavy metal violence, receiving all due and undue media attention, have involved suicides, church burnings, and homicides (Christe 2003; Moynihan and Søderlind 2003).

The heavy metal subculture, we argue, can be conceived as a homosocial environment because it comprises mostly of (white) men, who, further, typically exhibit high levels of aggression, rage, and anti-authority attitudes. The metal music community is known for a violently perceived style of dancing called moshing, where members push and bump into each other with much physical force in a manner that is typically thought of as highly masculine (Gruzelier 2007; Riches 2011, 2012, 2014; Wildberger and Farreras 2016). In its physically perhaps most radical form, moshing has evolved into "crowd killing" (mostly associated with the genre of hardcore, a hybrid of metal and punk), whereby fans at live shows wave their arms around in a fast windmill-like motion and kick their feet in the air in ostensible disregard of others (Luyten 2016). In part as a result of such practices, the subculture is often also seen as deviant, violent, and sexist by outsiders, which adds to its appearance of it being hypermasculine and misogynistic. The metal culture has also been described as hypermasculine because the majority of its fans and performers are men, who typically act in conventionally masculine ways (Glitsos 2020; Grant 1996; Recours et al. 2009; Swami et al. 2013; Weinstein 2000), with some evidence even indicating higher aggression and lesser regard for women (Rubin et al. 2001).

Besides the practice of moshing, which especially to outsiders may appear as extremely aggressive, heavy metal is at the same time, at least in some of its forms, also known for women engaging in "flashing" (exposing their breasts) at live shows, which has obvious sexual implications. Of course, there is no doubt that moshing is a much more common practice in heavy metal than flashing is or ever was, which is more generally practices across various forms of rock music. However, what is important for our research purposes is that we ask respondents about their perceptions of these two forms of concert activity because they are largely seen as inherently gendered. Moshing is especially popular at metal concerts of more aggressively sounding genres, such as thrash metal, death metal, and metalcore, while flashing, though much less common nowadays, still occurs at large popular (hard rock and) metal festivals in the United States, such as Ozzfest, Northern Invasion, Chicago Open Air, and Carolina Rebellion.

Both moshing and flashing, regardless of how much these practices actually occur, may give the heavy metal subculture the appearance of a place where women will be sexually objectified and disrespected because of these two activities' implied or assumed violent and sexual connotations, respectively. Also, while violent and/or sexually charged incidents in heavy metal may be relatively isolated, their portrayal in the media can be more impactful, especially toward outsiders of the genre. Only once does a media outlet have to report on a (presumably very rare) act of oral sex at a heavy metal show for it to be seen as reflective of the genre as a whole (Pasbani 2019). Even more problematic, of course, will it be when festival organizers summarily dismiss with any gender equity concerns when they assume women in heavy metal are less likely to be inspired to play their favorite music (Calleja et al. 2015).

If, and to the extent that, it is true that groups dominated by men are—all other conditions being equal—more likely to lead to instances of sexual assaults and violence against women, they are surely worthy of serious scholarly study to learn what fosters such gender-aggressive behaviors and, ideally, to be able to prevent or address conduct negative toward women. By example, research has found that sexual assaults on college campuses are, at least in part, attributed to the "party" environment, involving drinking and irresponsible behavior, that typically exists among students (Armstrong et al. 2006, p. 487). This condition parallels the environment at rock and metal concert venues, where drinking, loud music, and a general sense of chaos are not only accepted but encouraged as well. It is reasonable to suggest the notion that men who, for whatever reasons, already demonstrate misogynistic qualities are more likely to join hypermasculine groups such as the heavy metal subculture, further exacerbating gender-specific forms of hostility and aggression.

Relying on semi-structured interviews with self-identified fans of heavy metal, the adopted hermeneutic methodological strategy is appropriate and justified assuming that (subjective) views on what is perceived to be occurring in regard to the gender dynamics of their favorite musical genre can also affect the (objective) conditions of heavy metal's homosocial environment. By concrete example, although no broad statistical data on the total number of women among heavy metal fans across subgenres are available, a growing presence of women in the heavy metal community has been noted by virtually every single author in the field (as further explained in Chapter 2). This trend is also the primary reason why research, including our own, is being devoted to the issue. Our book seeks to make this contribution not quantitatively but by studying and seeking to understand the subjective opinions of metalheads themselves concerning these changes, an in-depth interpretive approach that is central to our work. As other scholars studying women in heavy metal have argued as well (Nordström and Herz 2013; Porrovecchio 2017), it is important to uncover what fans of the genre themselves experience and how they (subjectively) form their identity and (intersubjectively) construct that of others around them, rather than only adopt an external perspective of (objective) statistical conditions, even though the latter is, of course, needed as well.

A Look Ahead

A brief overview of the coming chapters may clarify what our book seeks to offer. In Chapter 2, we will explain the theoretical perspective of "doing gender" on the basis of a discussion of this variation of thinking in feminist sociology and related social science scholarship. Rooted in the tradition of women as the Other, we find it important to address issues of gender performativity and objectification in order to properly situate and develop our empirical research. We offer this sociological grounding not as a critique of but as a contribution to the broader realm of studies on popular culture and heavy metal.

In Chapter 3, we next specify our research questions on the heavy metal community on the basis of existing studies on the effects of hypermasculinity on women entering a variety of homosocial environments that traditionally have been dominated by men. We will specifically develop our research questions in terms of the hypermasculine nature of heavy metal and the changes that take place and the challenges that are presented, especially for women, in subcultures that become increasingly mixed-gender in character. As it would be foolish to assume the sociological orientation of our work would somehow absolve us from relying upon the existing academic literature outside of our immediate theme or discipline, we expressly, and at some length here, also ad-dress the relevant scholarship on heavy metal.

The next chapters of our book deal with the interview-based empirical re-search we conducted to uncover some important gender dynamics of heavy metal. After explaining our study's research questions and methods of analysis in Chapter 4, the three subsequent chapters discuss the central findings in terms of the central themes respondents brought out as their own (subjective) understandings of the heavy metal culture, whether (objectively) valid or not. Chapter 5 uncovers respondents' ideas concerning the status of the metalhead as an all-encompassing identity. The chapter will reveal the subjective dimen-sions of the metal identity, in particular the passion that is associated with the lifestyle and the related demarcation metalheads draw between insiders and outsiders. Chapter 6 takes on the specific theme of our work most directly by revealing how women in heavy metal are perceived to do gender in being a metal fan and in various forms of acting and playing, specifically moshing and flashing at live concerts. Chapter 7 addresses how metalheads identify and discuss questions of gender across various subgenres of heavy metal as well as the changes over time that they see have happened, are still happening, and/or should be happening.

Finally, in the concluding Chapter 8, we contemplate back on the theor-etical issues and research questions this book is grounded in to see what the gender dynamics in the world of heavy metal mean and imply in terms of their more or less lasting impact and significance. While the interviews of our study indicate it is empirically true that metalheads recognize that there has been a growing presence of women in heavy metal today, both as fans and as performers, not only the precise scope but especially the consequences and directions of these relatively new and still ongoing developments are not yet clear and fully understood. We will therefore again engage with the relevant literature on gender and heavy metal and the findings and perspectives offered in other studies. Concluding our work, we explore the possibilities as well as the obstacles in the development of a heavy metal feminism.

Chapter 2

DOING GENDER: A SOCIOLOGICAL PERSPECTIVE

This study theoretically relies on feminist perspectives of gender difference that identify a threefold dynamic of othering, objectification, and doing gender. Developing the notion of othering, we build on the classic work of Simone de Beauvoir (1952) concerning the notion of woman as the Other and, extending from this groundbreaking work, Judith Butler's (1990) concept of gender performativity. In turn inspired thereby, we rely on contemporary perspectives of objectification and doing gender. We find it important to explain this intellectual lineage of our perspective as rooted in classic work before it is applied in a contemporary context in order to adequately bring out the intellectual grounding of our work. Thus, by explaining the theory of our research at some length, this chapter seeks to avoid stepping into the world of heavy metal without a disciplinary basis and an appropriate model of analysis. Instead, we apply sociological concepts of gender in our study on women in heavy metal as a necessary basis for our empirical investigations. We believe these excursions, in this chapter and the next, are also justified for this book to reach its target audiences beyond expert scholars of gender, especially devotees of music and popular culture, as well as students and others interested in learning the foundations and objectives of sociology and gender studies.

Woman as the Other

Historically, theories of the social and cultural differences between men and women focused on the biological characteristics of, and differences between, the two sexes. At one time, biological perspectives asserted that men were the superior sex because of their larger physical size and greater physical strength. Such views were also justified by philosophical and, especially, religious ideas that held that women should be submissive to men. Although there are some early historical precursors to the development of feminist thought that would break with such sociologically unsustainable ideas (Madoo Lengermann and

Niebrugge 1998), it took as late as the middle of the twentieth century for feminist advances to be made in social thought. In 1949, feminist philosopher Simone de Beauvoir published the French-language version of her seminal work *The Second Sex* (de Beauvoir 1952), making her, even that recent in time, among the first to argue with great consequence that biological differences between men and women are not the cause of women's relative inequality and men's power.

In her groundbreaking book, de Beauvoir (1952) argues that women do not have a set destiny of subordination that would be created by their biological sex. Critiquing long-standing traditions in social theory, she argued against such ideas as those expressed by Friedrich Engels in his famous work *The Origin of the Family, Private Property and the State* (1884). Engels's theory postulated that as private property developed, it became necessary for men to pass on, upon their death, their belongings to their surviving heirs. The practice of monogamy developed to ensure that men could control their heirs to be their own biological children, resulting in a need to control women and their reproductive functions as one dimension of the control of private property.

De Beauvoir rejects the reductionist theory of Engels by stating that it undermines how important women's role of reproduction is in maintaining society. She also argues that if there were not already a human consciousness that created the category of the Other, it would not matter if men were the ones who took on leading roles in the economy and the development of capitalism (de Beauvoir 1952, p. 58). The consciousness of dominating the Other, instead, anticipates any functions associated with the control of private property. Even more profoundly, women also possess a consciousness of the Other and recognize themselves as such without much resistance. And when women do try to fight this notion, they do so typically in masculine ways (ibid., p. 129).

The options for women in a world dominated by men, such as it exists in the heavy metal community, then ironically cannot escape their status as the Other. The traditionally "feminine" woman will try to "catch" or, rather, get "caught by" a man by being sexually desirable, in the process of which she displays her body and herself to "present the inert and passive qualities of an object" (de Beauvoir 1952, p. 157). A more emancipated or "modern" woman, by contrast, will try to prove herself as equal to men by accepting their masculine values and attitudes (ibid., p. 718). In sum, what we learn from these insights, relevant until today, is that for women to be taken seriously, they must still portray masculine qualities and characteristics and, as it were, act as men or, at least, in relation to them.

Gender Performativity

American philosopher and gender theorist Judith Butler's (1990, 1993, 2004) work on gender and sexuality is heavily influenced by, and can be seen as an elaboration of, de Beauvoir's seminal ideas. Showing that de Beauvoir's original ideas are today anything but archaic, Butler in general sees the French philosopher's work as groundbreaking and still very useful, but also offers critiques to more fully capture the dynamics among gender, sex, and sexuality. For the purposes of this study, we specifically focus on Butler's work on gender performativity.

Gender performativity refers to the performance of gender in which men and women engage throughout their entire lives (Butler 1990). Biological sex is a starting point for gender performance, but the relationship between sex and gender is not deterministic. Transgendered individuals are a clear example of how biological sex is not, and cannot be, a concrete determinant of gender. Instead, it is through cultural cues and training practices, typically applied to people to whom the female sex is attributed, that gender becomes a learned performance. A crucial aspect of Butler's theory is that these performances take place in a "heteronormative matrix" that specifies the boundaries of what is masculine and what is feminine (Butler 1990, p. 136).

For gender performances to have actual implications, Butler (1990, p. 136) argues, they must be repeated constantly throughout social life. Then gender norms are (re)created and able to become dispersed throughout, and embedded in, culture (Brady and Schirato 2011, p. 46). By following such gender norms and viewing them as somehow natural, cultures can idealize heterosexuality as being biologically "normal" (Butler 1990, p. 135, 2004, p. 87). Butler's idea is similar to de Beauvoir's notion that women are the Other, next to men. Any other form of nonheteronormative sexuality becomes the Other and creates boundaries (Butler 1993, p. 9). Such boundaries are crucial for research on gender differences and the effects they can have on society's gender hierarchy and related power structures.

In her more recent book *Undoing Gender*, Butler (2004) looks at the body itself and discusses "cues" that distinguish between a woman's and a man's body. She raises the question of whether even these bodily aspects of life and living are determined by biological sex, or if it is a matter of adhering to cultural cues for what a man's and woman's body should look like. Butler relies on the example of intersex people to show that it is a combination of both cultural and biological factors, but that, socially, a clear binary structure is always presented. A person must be either man or woman to be appropriately "read" by society and, Butler (2004) writes, "bodily indicators are the cultural means by which the sexed body is read" (p. 87). This process informs, by example, why doctors typically will recommend that intersex babies undergo surgery to make them either male or female. Once the biological indicator is set, a culturally approved process of so-called gender marking can follow to maintain the binary categories of sex and gender by means of language that others women (from men), the female (from the male), and the feminine (from the masculine). From then on, the sex-based markers of gender can be acted upon in various manners of gender performativity. People will go about their entire lives "doing" these gender performances.

Objectification

The related concepts of the Other and gender performativity that were respectively developed by de Beauvoir and Butler have been taken up in various works of social science research on gender. Of interest in the present context is especially work on (self-)objectification, revealing the conditions of when both men and women view themselves as objects that are sexually and otherwise objectified, mostly in terms of women's bodies as an object of desire for the bodies of (heterosexual) men. The objectification of the sexes is historically rooted in myths surrounding biology and culture. This section will explain these processes of objectification in view of an analysis thereof in the world of heavy metal.

Historically, women were viewed as subordinate to men for reasons ranging from religious justifications to biological explanations related to the physical differences between male and female bodies (Nicholson 1994). The focus on biology and physicality enabled conditions of objectification to the point that such conditions would become internalized and adopted to one's view of self as both body and person. Self-objectification is the process of viewing one's body and self as a result of third-party definitions, typically coming from the opposite sex and mediated through the mass media (Newheiser et al. 2010, p. 657; Roberts and Gettman 2004). This objectification of the self can lead to psychological problems and negative emotions, especially on the part of women, although negative effects of self-objectification have been observed in men as well (Lorber and Martin 2007, p. 230; Newheiser et al. 2010, p. 658).

While the process of self-objectification and the mechanisms of objectifying others have traditionally been conceived as two separate, almost opposing processes, theoretical work adopting the notion of a "circle of objectification" proposes that objectification is a cycle that encompasses self-objectification, objectification of others, as well as comparisons among one another (Lindner et al. 2012). From this more complete and dialectical viewpoint, without question, all three factors should be considered when seeking to assess object-ification as a social phenomenon.

The most typical form of objectification that has been studied in the social sciences is sexual objectification, occurring when a body is viewed as an object of pleasure by another person, with all due repercussions. Feminists have argued that sexual objectification of women is a major factor contributing to the prevalence of sexual assault. When a woman is viewed as an object, it is easier for an attacker to justify their actions because a boundary is drawn between the self, as a human with needs, and the object that can satisfy those needs, even as their dynamics can be argued to center around power.

As a specific form of othering, sexual objectification can also have serious implications, for instance, on a legal level. The modern legal system is designed to enforce justice for all, but when a complex societal issue arises, it can bring about legal discrimination and lead to unequal treatment, with law functioning as a form of conflict itself. For example, sexual objectification impacts victim blaming in sexual assault cases, such as when an assaulted woman is said to have dressed in too provocatively a manner and is blamed for what happened to her as part of a process of dehumanization of the victim as an object of erotic desire (Henningsen et al. 2006; Rival et al. 1998).

Gender-based objectification permeates many spheres of society, especially through the functioning of the media as central socializing institutions. By example, feminist scholars have discussed the so-called male gaze to reveal how the visual media, most frequently television and cinema, will show women (and their bodies) from a viewpoint that is highly sexualized as objects of desire for men (Mulvey 1975). With such practices routinely applied, women become a sexual spectacle, displayed as an image that corresponds to men's sexualized fantasies. These displays lead to objectification because and inasmuch as both men and women see such images and start to internalize them as acceptable and thereby reinforce a gendered power structure.

Doing Gender

The notion of doing gender was introduced as a sociological concept in a 1987 article by Candace West and Don Zimmerman (1987), published in the journal *Gender and Society*. Since then, West and Zimmerman's article has become a mainstay in feminist scholarship (Messerschmidt 2009; West and Fenstermaker 1995; West and Zimmerman 2009), and the perspective of doing gender has become among the most popular and widely used ideas in the sociology of gender and related feminist perspectives in many different disciplines.

Developing their perspective, West and Zimmerman (1987) conceive of gender not merely as a construction by others but as "a routine, methodical, and recurring accomplishment [...] The 'doing' of gender is undertaken by women and men whose competence as members of society is hostage to its production. Doing gender involves a complex of socially guided perceptual, interactional, and micropolitical activities that cast particular pursuits as expressions of masculine and feminine 'natures'" (p. 126). While doing gender involves a performance on the part of men and women, the authors argue, this act of performing one's gender cannot be simply turned on and off from one situation to the next. Instead, it is something that individuals constantly adhere to in all environments. As such, the notion of doing gender contradicts Erving Goffman's (1979) concept of "gender display" inasmuch as doing gender assumes that gender categorization cannot be avoided. People create binary categories of gender (masculine and feminine) and apply them routinely in interactions (West and Zimmerman 1987, p. 133). Being categorized as a man or a woman not only leads to be able (or have) to do what is gender-appropriate but also implies there will be sanctions when something is done that is considered gender-inappropriate.

The concept of doing gender has in the meantime become so popular in theory and research that sociologists have come to use the concept at times only ceremoniously by referencing it but not actually applying or testing the underlying theoretical assumptions (Wickes and Emmison 2007). From a methodological viewpoint, it should be acknowledged that critics have argued that the method of interviewing (subjects) would be insufficient for testing purposes, and that the only valid way to test the theory is through observations of actual (objective) conduct (Wickes and Emmison 2007, p. 321). However, while we acknowledge that the generality of any theory of human conduct, in order to be tested, always needs to rely, absent the possibility of experimentation, on an examination or comparison of many cases of observable behavior, we argue that a qualitative approach, such as that adopted in our work on women in heavy metal, has advantages as well. A study using a relatively small number of semi-structured interviews as its main methodology cannot and should not be misused to test the general validity of the theory underlying the conceptual model of othering/gender performativity, objectification, and doing gender. However, lest a small sample be recognized to be used only for exploratory preliminary research or misused to infer generally applicable characteristics, our interview methodology can be relied on to lend valuable insights that are useful both to describe and, particularly, to understand the subjective dimensions of gender as one important set of factors that will also influence conduct. In the coming pages, we will apply these ideas to study fan perceptions on women in the heavy metal subculture.

Chapter 3

HYPERMASCULINITY AND HEAVY METAL

Applying the concept of doing gender to the world of heavy metal, a review of research in other areas of inquiry in which the notion of doing gender has been used will be helpful to situate, and develop a perspective useful for, our empirical investigations. This discussion will explain important dimensions of the homosocial form of hypermasculinity, even in societies expressly committed to gender equality, in order to advance our analysis. Specifically reviewed are examples of othering, objectification, and doing gender that have been researched in the workplace, in sports, and in a variety of more and less deviant subcultures. What these various settings have in common with the heavy metal community, we will show, is that they undeniably are, or at least traditionally were, dominated by men and hypermasculine as a result and, additionally, that they have undergone changes that today make them more gender-mixed in character than in the past. We review these issues along with a review of the relevant literature on heavy metal in order to situate our own empirical investigations.

Social Structure and Subculture: Hypermasculinity in Work and Play

The workplace and the sports world are both highly competitive social structures involving the pursuit of monetary and other rewards. With respect to workplaces historically dominated by men, research has uncovered gender issues posed by women taking up political offices, leadership positions in companies, and positions in jobs that have traditionally been defined as masculine because of the physicality and mentality that is held to be required, such as fire fighters, police officers, and the military. Women entering these hypermasculine environments have been shown to be criticized as less skilled and enterprising (Berg and Budnick 1986; Craig and Jacobs 1985; Davis et al. 2010; Guajardo 2016) and are subjected to gender marking to differentiate women's presumed aptitudes from those of men (Hauser 2011; Morgan and

Martin 2006). Although parental socialization of children has been found to reproduce gender inequities in work (Platt and Polavieja 2016), gender also becomes less salient, and negative stereotypes of women decrease over time, as more and more women enter such workplaces (Huffman 2013; Lawless 2004; Rosen et al. 2003).

Women in the world of sports can experience gender dynamics similar to the workplace. Research has generally found that women athletes are in the media portrayed in traditionally feminine terms and with an additional lack of awareness to their racial status in the case of minority athletes (Litchfield et al. 2018; Vincent et al. 2007; Wensing and Bruce 2003). Studies have found that women are marginalized in sports when and because they are assumed to be physically incapable of men's achievements (Anderson 2008; Ezzell 2009; Theberge 1993). Gender marking takes place in sports, notably in the media where women's sporting events are designated with an explicitly gendered label. For example, references will be made to "women's basketball" when women play the game, but simply to "basketball" when men's teams are involved (Messner et al. 1993, p. 125). Feeling challenged in all relevant respects, including physical strength (Sisjord and Kristiansen 2009), knowledge of the game (Theberge 1993), and athletic skills (Thorpe 2010), women in sports will respond and seek to counteract gender-based stereotyping by engaging in defensive othering (Ezzell 2009). Defensive othering takes place when women, rather than differentiating themselves from men, create a boundary between themselves and other women, against whom they will display masculine qualities in order to "win" in athletic terms. Women engage in defensive othering when and because they understand that they are not socially expected to be able to compete with men, to whom they continue to engage in a role understood as stereotypically feminine.

At the subcultural level, women have at times deliberately joined hypermasculine groups that involve lifestyles that offer an alternative to, and are sometimes even considered as deviant in, the wider social order. Women entering such subcultures face additional scrutiny for their participation in groups already considered deviant and develop coping strategies to fit in by adhering to traditional gender roles of femininity and/or, conversely, trying to be like "one of the guys" by performing masculinity (Fleetwood 2014; Lumsden 2010; Pilgeram 2007; Wolkomir 2012). These roles can rarely be done simultaneously and, instead, women will choose an appropriate strategy based on opportunity, needs, and desires.

An interesting and, for our purposes, the most significant example of the use of feminine and masculine techniques by women in subcultural groups is provided in research by Jody Miller about mixed-gender gangs (Miller 1998, 2001). Relying on semi-structured interviews of women with and without gang affiliation, Miller found that women will typically join a gang dominated by men to be protected from other men outside of the gang even though it subjected them to violence and semi-coerced sexual activity within the gang. Explicitly situated in the scholarship of doing gender, Miller's (2002) work serves as a direct inspiration for our research on women in heavy metal, not because we would argue that heavy metal subcultures are gangs but because both social forms have in their development experienced changes in a direction away from homosociality toward a (relative) mixed-gender status.

The degree of homosociality of the gang, Miller's research showed, greatly influences women's roles and conduct in the group. Hypermasculine gangs will rely on gender stereotypes and relate to women accordingly, protecting them as fragile members or attacking them as sexual prey. In mixed-gender gangs, these conditions are exacerbated because women and men compete among themselves and with one another. Women who exhibit masculine qualities in a mixed-gender gang, for instance, other themselves primarily, not from the men but from other women they consider to be feminine and overly sexualized. Some women, by example, choose to be initiated into the gang by being "beat in" by allowing themselves to be physically attacked by other gang members to prove their courage (just like the men) rather than being "sexed in" as other women do.

In sum, research on gender differences in the social structures of the workplace and in sports reveals that women in spheres dominated by men have to specially prove themselves and are not always taken seriously by the men with whom they work and/or compete. When women are employed in jobs or take part in sports that are traditionally hypermasculine, they are routinely othered and experience peculiarly high levels of doing gender because they are acutely subjected to gender marking. These conditions are seen to improve, however, as more women enter these realms and bring about more mixed and integrated conditions. Research on mixed-gender gangs similarly shows that women who can perform masculinity in hypermasculine terms are more likely to be accepted and less likely to be objectified, although they do so at a cost. Women who choose to employ femininity and still participate in the subcultural group do so because they think it is to their own advantage. Because and when clear distinctions are drawn between masculine and feminine women, defensive othering occurs when women displaying masculine qualities seek to show they are part of the hypermasculine group they aspire to belong to by distancing themselves from those women in the group who act in typically feminine ways. Inadvertently, but in a very real way, defensive othering thus leads to reaffirm (men's) existing stereotypes about how women should and can do their gender.

Studying Heavy Metal

Our discussion of the gender dynamics and processes of othering, objectification, and doing gender in various social structures and subcultures marked by hypermasculinity serves to explain important issues that can be examined to the world of heavy metal. Especially work on deviant subcultures will be revealed to be a useful source for our present study because cultural research on gender intimately relates to various issues, including gender itself, which studies on the heavy metal subculture also have addressed.

The scholarly study of popular culture and music has made tremendous strides in recent years after an initial slow start and resistance against such perspectives in sociology and related disciplines (Deflem 2017, pp. 11–17). For the purposes of this book, it will not be possible nor necessary to review all the scholarship that is now available in the study of heavy metal and in the broader field of (heavy) metal scholarship or metal (music) studies (Brown 2011; Spracklen et al. 2011). Suffice it to say that a sizable field of studies on heavy metal has been developing in recent decades, to wit the publication of several books and journal articles and the organization of dedicated conferences. Contemporary scholarship on various aspects of heavy metal includes a variety of monographs, anthologies, and graduate theses, along with an increasingly large number of journal articles (see the references listed in the bibliography and references throughout this book).

Although claiming its intellectual roots in the classic contributions by American scholars Deena Weinstein (1991) and Robert Walser (1993), metal music studies today is a primarily British affair, albeit with some international reach, that grew from within cultural studies (Spracklen et al. 2011). As a newly developing field that is as yet uncertain about its direction and foundations (as music studies or as an interdisciplinary area or as a multidisciplinary field), the contributions in heavy metal scholarship are of uneven quality and not intellectually unified. Although many of the writings in the field are of an empirical nature, they at times also engage in high-brow theoretical excursions (Mombelet 2005; Morris 2014, 2015). Only rarely appearing in mainstream academic outlets, the works of metal music studies all too often still seem to rely on the novelty aspect of taking on an off-beat area of study. At its worst, as a result, metal scholarship can be theoretically inadequate and empirically incoherent, making unwarranted extrapolations on the basis of mere interpretations of one band's lyrics or video (Digioia 2016a; Sollee 2015) or unjustifiable generalizations from small data sets (Hill 2016a). Other such area studies falling considerably short of acceptable research standards unverifiably present their insider experiences as ("autoethnographic") scholarship (Shadrack 2021), resort to stale meta-analysis of others' works (Helfrich

2017), and fail to credit earlier work that served as a clear but hidden inspiration (Doucette 2018).

Some of the difficulties in the development of metal music studies as an independent field of study claiming legitimacy have been recognized by at least some of its practitioners (Savigny and Schaap 2018). And, indeed, the relatively unbalanced development of abstract theory and empirical research is not uncommon, nor necessarily problematic, for a relatively new and still developing area of scholarship and need not lead to its total rejection. However, the scholarly study of heavy metal needs justification beyond the mere existence or popularity of its theme. For so-called metal scholars to properly recognize that the examined cultural and structural aspects of the heavy metal community reflect broader societal patterns and dynamics, their research activities need to be framed as part of a broader field of area studies, such as popular culture or (popular) music, or be conducted from within the existing disciplinary perspectives of the social and behavioral sciences. For otherwise the specialty scholars of metal music studies—relying on their own association and journal (the MetalStudies website)—would act as gatekeepers to exclude all work, not matter how valid or valuable, because its authors might not have been previously heard of. In any case, an area of study that purports to be conscious of itself will flourish among other academic fields only if it also attains consciousness and recognition from others. As Robert Merton (1972) argued in his work in the sociology of science, a relatively modest (middle-range) approach of theory construction should therefore eventually also enable a useful integration of general theory with empirical research. Only then, as in the case of metal music studies and other thematically focused scholarship, can useful epistemological and ontological claims potentially develop from a community of scholars' claims of solidarity.

What is important for the present purposes is that scholarly work on heavy metal has typically been conducted from the viewpoint of the study of a nonmainstream, more or less deviant, or, at least, variant subculture surrounding music that is associated with youth culture, identity, class, and gender (Gaines 1998; Verden et al. 1989; Walser 1993). This focus makes sense given the musical form's general rebelliousness, the rowdiness of its fanbase, and some of its at times relatively infamous countercultural personae. Correspondingly, research has shown that the heavy metal subculture attracts people, especially adolescents, who are less likely to have higher education (Hällsten et al. 2019), feel alienated from mainstream society (Arnett 1996; Friesen 1990; Haenfler 2010), feel negatively toward authority (Swami et al. 2013), and enjoy their participation in the heavy metal subculture as a disalienating politics of resistance (Halnon 2006; Hoad 2016). These findings strengthen the notion that heavy metal is a subculture because its members expressly distance themselves, in their actions and beliefs, from mainstream popular culture and society (Fine and Kleinman 1979). The rebelliousness and sense of nonconformity toward the mainstream that drives participation in the heavy metal community will be amplified for women as they, by the very act of becoming a metalhead, also break gender expectations, a condition that is even more pronounced in more traditional cultures (Horton 2021).

As a result of the focus on heavy metal as a subculture for the alienated, questions surrounding identity, belonging, and well-being are key issues that scholarship on heavy metal has devoted all due attention to (Blott 2021; Larsson 2013; O'Hagan 2021a, 2021b; Snell and Hodgetts 2007). Participants in the heavy metal community, besides the casual snakeskin cowboys and weekend warriors, do not merely define themselves as fans of heavy metal music, but as metalheads, fully committed to the music, the lifestyle, and the culture. Not surprisingly, as a musical genre, heavy metal has generally, that is, by the mainstream majority of society, been found to be one of the most disliked genres of popular music (Bryson 1996). Moral panics related to heavy metal have not surprisingly taken place because of the music's perceived dangers, with charges of promoting suicide (Stack, Gundlach, and Reeves 1994), of contributing to violence such as school shootings (Schiller 2012), and of referencing lyrically and otherwise to themes of evil, Satanism, self-harm, and depression (Blott 2021; Granholm 2019; Haenfler 2010; Mombelet 2005), for which reason the genre has been singled out for control and censorship (Deflem 2020). Yet, precisely because of such reactions, whether they are valid or not (Baker and Brow 2016), metalheads are fervently dedicated to the heavy metal subculture and its contempt for order and civility.

Unlike what has begun to transpire in most recent years, scholars of heavy metal traditionally did not focus as much on gender as a separate theme worthy of special consideration but, instead, devoted attention to gender-related issues in connection with other topics such as identity, self, and group formation. The conventional findings center on heavy metal's predominance of men and masculinity and the general lack of participation by women, except mostly as sexual objects in the sexist songs and other practices of metal music. As active participants, women have traditionally largely been considered a key constituent primarily only of the so-called hair metal movement of the 1980s—the genre Deena Weinstein (2000, pp. 45–48) calls "lite metal"—when women fans flocked to live shows to adore their favorite "glamor boys" of commercial metal, precisely at a time when hypermasculinity and sexism were central characteristics of the scene (Denski and Sholle 1992; Heritage 2016; Sloat 1998). Whereas women musicians in heavy metal in those days were mostly seen as a novelty at best and sexually harassed at worst (Caporale 2018), the role of women as metal fans was largely one of doting devotees and groupies in the tradition of 1970s arena rock (Howe and Friedman 2014; Howe et al. 2015). Although the notion of the groupie as subservient to the sexual desires of the masculine gods of metal may not have accurately reflected negotiated realities between women and their idols, the groupie stereotype may nonetheless have contributed to hinder the reception of women in heavy metal as full and equal participants in the community (Forrest 2010). The recent resurgence of commercial glam metal will, in any case, face different gender conditions today than those that prevailed several decades ago (Kores 2020; Kummer 2017).

It is noteworthy that several of the best-known contemporary scholars doing research on heavy metal in relation to gender (and other themes) are women, as examples throughout this book will reveal. In fact, the visible presence of women in the study of heavy metal might itself be seen as a form of doing gender that could also positively contribute to the reception and acceptance of women in the subculture (Hickam and Wallach 2011). This situation is less ironic as it may at first appear as these scholars are typically also metal fans (and even amateur musicians), who are well positioned, therefore, to experience and reflect on the subculture's homosociality and hypermasculinity. Of course, the insider position as fan must make way for the outsider role as scholar to produce sound academic work and avoid getting lost in meaningless arguments about a scholar's purported lack (or mastery) of knowledge of heavy metal music, such as when, in the case of gender, an author's understanding of "the benefits of metallic involvement for women" is claimed to be "a little too optimistic" (Hill 2016c). To be useful and achieve academic recognition, instead, metal fans doing research on various aspects of their community need to rely on a clear scholarly perspective to fruitfully analyze what they might have learned from, but also might have to question about, their fandom.

Heavy metal has indeed often been described as not just being dominated by men but as distinctly and highly masculinist in terms of a discourse shaped by patriarchy (Walser 1993, pp. 108–36; Weinstein 2000, pp. 102–6). Heavy metal was traditionally found to appeal mostly to men who hold conventional gender stereotypes and display rather negative, sexist attitudes toward women (St. Lawrence and Joyner 1991). Whether men who are sexist are more likely to be attracted to heavy metal or whether such attitudes are the result of their exposure to the subculture is not entirely clear, but might reasonably be explained by a dialectical dynamic. In view of the development of heavy metal from the 1970s until today, important variations also exist among the musical style's many subgenres, which range from relatively conventional hard rock to more so-called extreme forms of heavy metal. For example, men have traditionally been found to favor thrash, speed, and power metal genres, which are louder, faster, and generally more aggressive in sound and style, while women mostly only favored more commercially oriented heavy metal (Weinstein 2000, p. 299). In the meantime, however, with the enormous stylistic and cultural differentiation of heavy metal music (as music) as well as with the increasing role women play in music and in culture at large, these gender dynamics have become far more complex than this traditional perspective once indicated (Hoad 2016; Jocson-Singh 2016).

The initially only secondary attention to women in heavy metal is not surprising because it was largely the result of the homosociality of the metal scene itself and, of course, of sociology and academia as well. Conforming to expectations of the style and culture of heavy metal, the metal community has traditionally been described as hypermasculine in terms of the relatively aggressive behavior of its fans and the general lack of women participants. Heavy metal aggression, by example, has been associated with fans moshing (in mosh pits) at live metal concerts (Epp 2019; Palmer 2005; Riches 2011, 2012, 2014). Moshing appears to be nonsensically violent to outsiders, while insiders who engage in the practice typically do so in a playful manner and on the basis of a set of rules and etiquette to ensure that no one is injured. Sociologist Deena Weinstein, one of the leading experts in the study of heavy metal, compares moshing to people riding bumper cars, denoting it is meant to be a fun way of smashing into each other (Weinstein 2000, p. 229).

Moshing has also been argued to be distinctly gendered as it poses special issues of physicality along with cultural (dis)approval for women (Riches 2012; Riches et al. 2013). Experimental research by psychologists Jared Wildberger and Ingrid G. Farreras (2016) found that women were more likely than men to receive indirect rather than direct help when they fell down in a mosh pit, showing that other moshers were more likely to conceive of the men as fellow moshers rather than as innocent bystanders who accidentally were caught in the mosh. Metal scholar Gabby Riches therefore describes moshing as a "prime example" of how "heavy metal represents itself as a haven of male homosocial interactions," even though and when women participate as well (Riches 2014, p. 88). More broadly, although a relatively small number of women have historically also been found to be attracted to heavy metal because they, similarly to the men, felt an alienation to mainstream society, a gender hierarchy has often been observed among those participating in the metal scene in a manner that mirrored dominant gender conventions (Krenske and McKay 2000, p. 279).

Gender in Heavy Metal

For reasons formally similar to the initial lack of attention to gender in the study of heavy metal, explicitly gender-oriented studies on heavy metal have in recent years become much more prevalent. As references to the literature throughout this book will show, the topic of gender in heavy metal has, in fact, become among the more popular themes in contemporary research, much like it also has in a multitude of other areas in social science scholarship. In the case of heavy metal, the power of gender as a popular theme of contemporary reflection has even attracted research on such esoteric topics as gender differences in physiological reactivity while listening to metal music (Becknell et al. 2008) and the perceived attractiveness of website hosts playing heavy metal as background music (Yang and Li 2014). This popularity of heavy metal and gender in scholarship mirrors similar conditions in popular culture, as testified, for instance, by the embrace of the imagery, if not always the music, of heavy metal by mainstream performers such as Lady Gaga (Deflem 2015) and the use—or abuse—of heavy metal T-shirts among many of today's (women) celebrities (Magnotta 2017; Pasbani 2017).

Sociologically relevant research has generally shown that important changes have taken place in recent years with respect to the generally observed under-representation of women in the heavy metal community. Particularly influential to stimulate this research has been the appearance of not only women fans (which some metal genres were already able to attract some decades ago) but also women musicians participating in heavy metal bands (Glitsos 2020; Ritlop 2020). As a result of their active presence, the contemporary women of heavy metal essentially "defy the stereotype of women as groupies" and assert their position in a now increasingly more mixed-gender subculture (Haenfler 2010, p. 61). As these changes are still very much ongoing, research on the role of gender in heavy metal remains in need of continued development and rethinking, thematically as well as in methodological and theoretical respects.

What are some of the findings and insights that recent studies on gender and heavy metal, especially concerning the position and role of women, have taught us? From a methodological viewpoint, it is interesting to note that many of the recent studies on gender and heavy metal have relied on interviews and ethnographic methods of data collection, not rarely conducted by scholars whose work is influenced by their participation as fans and/or performers in the heavy metal community (Hill 2016a; Krenske and McKay 2000; Porrovecchio 2017; Savigny and Sleight 2015; Shadrack 2017; Vasan 2011, 2016). Such works therefore may run the risk of a lack of necessary detachment to produce valid scholarship (Savigny and Schaap 2018). Yet, providing that a clear framework and methodology of study is relied upon and consistently applied, relying on in-depth research of women's (own) experiences and perceptions as participants in heavy metal can also have the advantage of coming to a better understanding of what it is like to be a woman fan in an environment that is routinely presented as sexist, especially in the media. We hope to achieve this scholarly requirement by means of reliance on the theory of doing gender and the qualitative methodology of our study.

Focusing on some of the empirical results of recent research on heavy metal women, the broadest findings indicate not only that there are more women present in heavy metal today, both as fans and as performers, but generally also that their experiences are more positive as active and respected participants. Although exact numbers are missing, there is no doubt that there are more women in heavy metal today than ever before, even in such extreme genres as death metal and grindcore (Barron 2013; Overell 2012; Schaap and Berkers 2014), and that the subculture as a whole can therefore no longer be simply described as hegemonically masculine (Scott 2016). Today's women of heavy metal are also more diverse in the multiple roles they take on, both as performers, such as singers of so-called female-fronted metal bands (Chaker and Heesch 2016), and as instrumentalists, as well as active fans, engaged in the usual behaviors of listening to the music, dressing as a metalhead, and going to shows to enjoy the music along with everybody else. In some genres of heavy metal, such as contemporary symphonic metal and folk metal, the presence of women has almost become mandatory. Representations of conventional gender roles in the lyrics of traditional heavy metal rooted in classic rock (Friesen and Helfrich 1998) have since also made way for a more complex constellation of themes. More often than before sung by women, today's metal songs address a broader range of issues rooted in realism, hyperrealism, and transgressive fantasy (DiGioia 2016b; Flansburg 2021). The music thereby seeks to challenge the gendered realities of the heavy metal subculture by lyrically reflecting upon them (Bolay 2019).

The current status of women in heavy metal has not only been influenced by the growing presence of women in the subculture but has, similar to the position of women in society at large, also benefited from the changing ideas on masculinity that exist among men. Deena Weinstein (2016) has in this respect argued that a measure of gender play is at work inasmuch as different kinds of masculinity exist in heavy metal, depending on the time period and subgenre of the musical style and culture. Specifically, the invidious and exclusionary masculinity of 1970s classic metal and the hypermasculinity of 1980s thrash metal have by now given way to a broader variety of gender cultures, such as the broken masculinity of 1990s nu metal and the romantic masculinity of twenty-first century goth metal. Such changing and more diverse developments from within the community (of the men of heavy metal) are potentially also beneficial to women's possibilities to do gender with less constraints.

At the same time, as gains no doubt have been made, the contemporary situation of women in heavy metal remains ambiguous, as boundaries have been discovered to persist in women's participation in the scene as equals (Savigny and Sleight 2015; Vasan 2011, 2016). Despite recent positive changes for women metalheads, most research shows, there still exists a divide between women and men in the heavy metal scene, and questions remain over the meaning of these changes and how men interact with women and react to their growing presence (Porrovecchio 2017). No matter the gains, in straightforward terms it must be said that heavy metal remains a largely, though no longer exclusively, homosocial environment dominated by men. And the contemporary resurgence of 1980s commercial hair metal (a style of music that has always drawn many women fans) is nowadays not even considered ("real") metal at all, but a form of nostalgic entertainment for older fans, with an additional, somewhat satirical appeal to a younger audience (Griffin 2014). The persistence of masculinity in heavy metal also intersects with race (Dawes 2012) and class (Brown and Griffin 2014), with lower- to middle-class men predominant among metalheads, so that conventional values of gender and sexism are reproduced and maintained.

It is of special interest to our work here to note that some scholars studying gender and heavy metal have, in more or less elaborate ways, also discussed the notion of doing gender (Berkers and Schaap 2018; Krenske and McKay 2000; Miller 2016, 2017; Vasan 2011). Especially interesting to learn from these studies, as the discussion to our findings will further reveal (see Chapter 8), are observations on the essentially ambivalent nature of the status of women in heavy metal. For instance, explicitly relying on the doing gender perspective of Candace West and her coauthors (West and Zimmerman 1987; West and Fenstermaker 1995), sociologists of music and art Pauwke Berkers and Julian Schaap (2018) studied women involved in the production of heavy metal music to find that they are marked by a "double-edged sword" of femininity as women producing metal music receive greater attention but also, because of their femininity, might not be taken as seriously as the men of metal. Likewise, and thematically closer to our investigation of fan perceptions of heavy metal, Susanna Nordström and Marcus Herz (2013) found, similar to our study on the basis of interviews, that women metalheads need to perform gender more than men do, because they are typically forced to abide by the (hyper)masculine values of the subculture. Similar such dualities will indeed be revealed in our research as well.

Implications

The findings from recent research on gender and heavy metal substantiate the notion that, as in the homosocial worlds of the workplace, sports, and gangs, women entering and participating in the social structure and subculture of heavy metal have to do gender and engage in defensive othering in conventional terms of masculinity and femininity (Krenske and McKay 2000). As contemporary research has shown, women in heavy metal must typically therefore adopt and adhere to or, at the very least, take into account masculinity in order to purposely fight and resist the values and actions associated therewith and practice a new, more authentically understood form of femininity (Nordström and Herz 2013; Turbé 2016). Even as heavy metal, especially perhaps some of its most so-called extreme genres such as death metal and black metal, presents a space where women do not have to conform to society's standards of femininity, but can, at least temporarily, resist gender-based conventions (Patterson 2016a, 2016b; Shadrack 2017), there remains a distinct need to continue to do gender on men's terms (Berkers and Schaap 2018; Krenske and McKay 2000).

The parallels that can be noted in the findings of gender studies in the workplace, sports, and subcultural groups as compared to the heavy metal subculture will inform our empirical analysis in no small part because of the formal similarities that exist among these environments. Of course, the world of heavy metal is not work (but play), not deliberately competitive (but communal), and not an organized gang (but a loose-knit community). Yet, the similarities among these settings are striking in terms of important aspects of gender because all are, albeit in varying degrees, traditionally homosocial in their structure and hypermasculine in their cultural dispositions. Additionally, these spheres of social life have in common that they have all been affected by a growing presence of women.

Especially in view of the increasing participation of women in heavy metal as a subculture that to some extent is also considered deviant, we expect strong similarities with the gender dynamics that Miller (1998, 2001) observed in gangs. Like gangs, the heavy metal subculture is traditionally homosocial, dominated by men, hypermasculine, and known for the occasionally aggressive behavior among its members. These characteristics can lead to a distinctly hierarchical structure, whereby the men are placed higher than the women based solely on assumed gender characteristics. Such gender-based hierarchy can lead to a victimization of women on multiple levels, including violent behavior and sexual assault, not as a quasi-natural outcome but as a form of control.

Heavy metal concerts are known for being loud and rowdy. Mosh pits involve a level of physical aggression that, it can be argued, can provide a setting where women could be victimized, especially as and when they are outnumbered by men. Such problematic behavior damaging to women would be similar to the sexual aggressions that exist in mixed-gender gangs. While extreme incidents are usually isolated events, they are examples of how a hypermasculine environment, in combination with other factors, can be less than hospitable to women members. Such conditions should not, of course, lead to automatically conclude that sexual assault will be more common in heavy metal. Yet, it is important to consider that (heterosexual) assault is—all other conditions being equal—more likely on numerical grounds alone when more women are present in an environment that was traditionally dominated by men, especially when it is characterized by hypermasculine values. Variable conditions of the integration of women across different genres of heavy metal will play an important role here as well.

Moreover, both gangs and the heavy metal subculture are characterized by a relatively sharp separation between insiders and outsiders in terms of an us-versus-them dichotomy. In a gang, the outsiders involve rival gangs and society at large. The sharp boundary among rivaling gangs justifies initiation practices to prove loyalty and earn membership. In the heavy metal subculture, similar boundaries exist within the various subgenres of metal, each claiming authenticity within, and separation from, the outside world of mainstream society from which metalheads feel alienated. Both subcultures are also marked by distinguishable characteristics of clothing and style to visibly display and reveal identity and membership. Inasmuch as gangs and the heavy metal scene are dominated by men, such practices of belonging place pressures on women seeking entry as they may need to specially prove themselves because of their gender.

Finally, the manner in which women have over the years taken up a more active role as members to form mixed-gender gangs again parallels the heavy metal scene in having become a gender-wise more diverse environment. While there is some disagreement over whether heavy metal is inherently masculine and/or accurately presented as sexist in the media as well as in scholarship (see Chapter 8), heavy metal has traditionally, since its historical origins, been masculine and dominated by men, so that the growing presence of women can lead to resistance in the form of defending one's exclusive space. It is clear from recent research that the women who have successfully entered the heavy metal world today are still confronted with conditions of hypermasculinity. Invoking Butler's (1990) theory of performativity, recent research has shown that women in heavy metal need to carefully balance between "acting like a man" and still "looking like a woman" (Nordström and Herz 2013; Riches 2015). This in-between condition may leave metal women insufficiently masculine for the heavy metal subculture and insufficiently feminine for mainstream society. Generally confronted with masculine values (Savigny and Sleight 2015), metal women have to continually engage in a balancing act by navigating their gender with those of others, at times even leading them to a willingness to tolerate outright sexism (Vasan 2011).

The ongoing changes in the world of heavy metal pose an interesting condition concerning the extent and nature of the advancement of women in today's metal as compared to other musical styles. Consider the case of alternative rock, a form of popular music that is also—albeit less—loud and wild, but which generally adopts a more serious and supposed politically and socially conscious approach. In the world of alternative hard rock, the gendered lines of heterosexual dominance can be more blurred. As both men and women in alternative hard rock sought to reject the idea of the groupie, a measure of gender fluidity is present in that women can act in semi-sexual ways with one another (Schippers 2000, p. 750; see also contributions in Heesch and Scott 2016). This less conventional approach to gender boundaries in alternative rock can be attributed to its lower degree of homosociality as the music style is less dominated by men than is the world of heavy metal.

It is therefore on theoretical grounds astute to wonder if, with respect to gender, contemporary heavy metal is becoming in reality what the world of alternative rock has already aspired to be as an ideal, irrespective of the fact that politically charged content is present in both musical forms. After all, notwithstanding such influential heavy metal songs as "War Pigs" by Black Sabbath, "Peace Sells" by Megadeth, or "One" by Metallica (all anti-war songs), as well as the varying political objectives of metal genres across different societies (Epp 2017; Goossens 2019), politically oriented leanings are far more prevalent in other forms of popular music such as folk, punk, and alt-rock, where such concerns are also more readily embraced by fans and performers alike (Spracklen 2013). Nonetheless, though its participants would shudder to think they have anything in common, musically or otherwise, the heavy metal subculture might as such become more akin to alternative rock from the viewpoint of issues relating to hypermasculinity and doing gender.

Chapter 4

INTERROGATING HEAVY METAL: FAN PERCEPTIONS ON GENDER

To address the introduced issues of gender in the heavy metal subculture, the empirical component of this book relies on interviews with 10 women and 10 men who identify as fans of heavy metal. In keeping with the subjectivist approach of our examination, we did not apply an external standard to establish who qualifies as a fan of heavy metal, but instead let the respondents make that determination themselves. Because the focus of our work is on perceptions concerning women in the metal community, it is important to note that the interviews were conducted by the first author of this book, a woman, who herself also participates in the world of metal, a genre of music the second author has been involved with since the transformation from hard rock to heavy metal from the late 1960s onwards. The interviews were conducted with approval from the Institutional Review Board at the University of South Carolina, and both authors successfully passed required training for research involving human subjects.

It goes without saying that the small sample size of the interviews cannot lay claim the criteria of a random selection of research subjects upon which generalizable conclusions could be reached to a broad population. However, by selecting an equal number of men and women, we are able to reach conclusions on the critical role that gender plays in the opinions of heavy metal fans about their favorite music community. Furthermore, as our study is oriented at an adequate understanding of subjective experiences rather than an explanation of objective conditions, the findings derived from the interviews are illustrative of relevant issues in the sociology of gender and the dynamics of doing gender to bring out subjective but relevant meaning (Westmarland 2001).

Interviews

Because of the focus on the evolving status of women in a traditionally masculine world, an equal number of 10 men and 10 women were purposely selected to be interviewed. Importantly, we hereby do not rely on sex rather than gender as categories of selection, let alone address the question of the relationship between gender identity and biological sex. Instead, all respondents self-identified as a man or a woman, terms that they could (and, as results will show, indeed did) define themselves as a matter of gender and/or sex.

The interview respondents range in age from 18 to 49 years. Nineteen of the respondents live in various parts of the United States, including the states of New York, California, Ohio, and South Carolina, and one is from France. Two of the participants identified as Asian, one as Hispanic/White, and the remaining as White. The number of concerts attended by the study participants range from one to over four hundred. Five of the interviews were conducted face to face, one took place by phone without permission to record, and the remaining 14 interviews were conducted online by email or via Facebook chat. Ideally, all interviews would have been conducted face to face to assure a more interactive in-depth approach, but it turned out to be unexpectedly difficult to find respondents and, subsequently, to come to an agreement on a time and method for the interviews. It is interesting of the nature of the heavy metal culture itself to say a few more words about these methodological challenges.

The five participants who were interviewed face to face were found with the help of a heavy metal music DJ of a local University of South Carolina radio station, who also books weekly metal shows at local bars and is very involved in the local music scene. The DJ helped us look for fans interested in participating in this study via his Facebook page and by word of mouth, through which seven people contacted the interviewer. The interviews with the first two of these respondents (both of them men) were not withheld for data analysis, because they did not produce useful results. As the interviewer was soon to discover, her decision to adopt a professional style of dress during these early interviews produced an adverse effect in that the respondents, rather than thinking the study was a serious academic venture, felt like they were being investigated by an outsider. The remaining five face-to-face interviews ran smoothly as the interviewer had wisely changed to her (not unusual) outfit of ripped jeans, combat boots, and metal T-shirt.

Because not more respondents were found via the local metal DJ, undergraduate students in selected sociology classes at the University of South Carolina were asked to confidentially identify the genre of music they liked the most, hoping to find more local metalheads. Yet, among the roughly 175 students who were polled, not a single fan of heavy metal was identified. The differences that exist in the world of popular music in terms of region, possibly in connection with level of education, were clearly not to our advantage.

We next decided to identify fans at heavy metal concerts to serve as respondents. Over the course of the initial data collection period, the first author attended three metal concerts, in Kentucky, North Carolina, and South

Carolina. Even though she approached several people at all three shows, not one person was found willing to do an interview. At a Slipknot concert in Kentucky, the interviewer wore relatively elaborate makeup depicting her face as a ghoulish skull, befitting die-hard fans of the band (among whom she counts herself), but found that it only seemed to irritate most women fans who were approached. One woman (out of four women who were approached) told her, to "go on with your girly shit!" At another South Carolina metal show, featuring the nu metal band Mushroomhead, the interviewer decided to dress in a more traditional metal outfit (black jeans, black combat boots, black metal T-shirt) and approached even more concert attendants. But fans reacted wearily and seemed to think the request was a scam of sorts and refused to be interviewed. One man initially agreed to an interview, but later withdrew because he said he was too busy.

Finally, the authors decided to contact acquaintances who are known as fans of heavy metal from among their respective involvements and experiences in music and asked them to serve as respondents and/or help us find additional participants. Primarily via contacts on the Twitter and Facebook accounts of the second author, this method went more smoothly and produced several additional respondents. To assure unbiased results, we made sure to only interview people the interviewer had never met, spoken with, or otherwise been in touch with. Using these methods and on the basis of snowball sampling with the first round of participants, it was eventually possible to conduct a total of 20 interviews with 10 men and 10 women.

The five face-to-face interviews took place in the public location, a coffee shop. Along with the phone interview, these interviews typically lasted around thirty minutes and were conducted in a semi-structured manner. The interviews would ideally have been longer in duration but, absent any monetary incentives for the study participants, they were kept at more reasonable length so as not to burden the respondents too much and still be able to elicit useful data. An interview guide containing a list of questions was used (by the interviewer alone) to make sure all necessary information was covered while at the same time allowing for leads from the respondents themselves so that the interviews could go in a different, unexpected direction, as is demanded by this methodology (Bernard 2013, p. 182). The 14 online interviews were conducted by first sending the participants the questions from the interview guide and subsequently following up on their responses for additional explanation and clarification.

Rather than relying on a survey, the data of this study were collected by means of semi-structured interviews because of the specific type of information this project sought to uncover. Indeed, in order to understand the experiences of the participants, we were interested in knowing their subjective interpretations concerning the gender dynamics in heavy metal. Nondirective informal interviewing provides the best means to adequately understand the behaviors, states of mind, and interpretations of events of the participants themselves (Morgan and Martin 2006; Pilgeram 2007; Wolkomir 2012). Admittedly, in view of the choices we had to make to conduct some interviews by means of email or Facebook chat, certain limitations were imposed on the depth that could be reached. While probing for further information could obviously be conducted more readily in the face-to-face interviews, the written interviews were followed up with a one-time request for additional clarifications. Although some comparability issues may exist between the written and verbal interviews, it is striking that some of the written responses to the interview questions provided among the most detailed information.

Because of the focus of research on women in the hypermasculine world of heavy metal, we recognize that the interviews, especially with women respondents, might involve discussions that are of a personal nature, possibly leading to a measure of response bias. However, given the interviewer's own status as a woman researcher who also possesses considerable knowledge (as a participant) of the heavy metal culture, the interviews were conducted using an appropriate type of language and repertoire, as feminist research indeed requires (DeVault 2002). Especially the expertise of heavy metal by both authors was helpful to identify respondents, while the first author's knowledge of the metal subculture was particularly useful during the interviews to avert participants being suspicious about why their subculture was being studied. Especially when a participant needed reassurance, the interviewer revealed her own participation in the metal subculture to give herself credibility and invoke more honest and valid answers (Singleton and Straits 2010, p. 380).

The relative degree of our subjectivity as researchers could have played a role in this study because of its qualitative design (Glesne 2011, p. 151). The interviewer's stance as a feminist metal fan might have impacted the direction of the data collection, but this will be mitigated by the study's theoretical foundations and the critical feedback both authors of this work provided one another. We also sought to keep our not always overlapping experiences and subjective dispositions, both on music and on gender, deliberately separate from this study. Our own fandom of the music could be bracketed by not focusing primarily on the music itself, but on the culture and, of course, by reliance on theory, methodology, evidence, and the literature with which we engage. Nonetheless, it is possible that respondents were not always honest, especially not the men, who may have been less forthright than they would have been to a man (especially one who is not a metalhead) interviewing them.

The online interviews by e-mail and Facebook may have had an advantage by lacking any face-to-face pressure about how respondents could have perceived any interviewer reaction to statements about women in the sub-culture. Most apparent, however, was that the respondents during the face-to-face interviews often asked if the interviewer herself was a metal fan and that they were visibly more at ease once they knew they were not interro-gated by an outsider who was out to ridicule them. Remarkably, especially the men among the respondents would sometimes ask very specific information about the interviewer's involvement and knowledge of heavy metal, such as by asking her about the shows she had been to and the bands she likes. As we will see from the results of our study, these respondents may thereby have already demonstrated a central finding of our analysis, because it suggests that the (woman) interviewer had to prove herself as a fan toward the men respondents.

Research Questions and Data Analysis

Consistent with the theoretical framework we specified about the role of gender in homosocial groups, the research questions that were explored in the interviews pertain to the overall characteristics of the heavy metal subcul-ture and, more in particular, the place and role of women therein. In terms of gender, we rely on the threefold model of othering/gender performativity, objectification, and doing gender as applied to a traditionally hypermasculine subculture in which women have increasingly become involved.

Specifically, the research questions of this study are organized in the fol-lowing five categories:

1. What does it mean to the respondent to be a fan of heavy metal?
2. What are the self-reported reasons for joining the heavy metal subculture?
3. Do respondents feel that women in heavy metal are discriminated against and, if so, do the respondents attribute it to women's minority status in the subculture?
4. Do women respondents describe experiences of being othered and/or objectified? Are the men among the study participants aware of women's experiences? Do opinions on the gender dynamics in the heavy metal subculture differ between men and women?
5. What are respondents' attitudes about the possible implications of the practices of moshing and flashing relative to the status of women fans in the heavy metal subculture? Do respondents' attitudes relate to descrip-tions of women doing their gender and/or undoing their gender?

On the basis of the strategy of a "checklist of major points" (Bradburn et al. 2004, p. 118), a total of 16 interview questions, besides three demographic data, were drawn up to answer the identified research questions (see the appendix). The questions were designed to be at first broad in order to identify subjective orientations toward metal and also to see if the study participants would already mention gender issues when asked general questions about the heavy metal subculture. The general questions were content-wise based on the themes retrieved from the literature on the heavy metal subculture, exploring the meaning of being a metal fan and designed to elicit general descriptive responses from the participants. The subsequent interview questions were targeted specifically at gender issues in the subculture. The final part of the interviews, addressed in the last two interview questions, was specifically meant to uncover fans' thoughts about moshing and flashing. Women participants were asked the same questions as the men in order to better be able to compare the findings.

The interview questions were explored as an interview guide, not as a formal questionnaire, to ensure that specific topics were covered in a generally specified order (Bernard 2013, p. 182). The questions guided the conversations with the participants during the face-to-face and phone interviews. This style of interviewing flowed more like an informal conversation than a formally prestructured survey. This approach has the advantage to produce a more in-depth discussion that provides more fruitful information on the subjective experiences of the participants, the primary aim of this study. The first few interview questions were also purposely very general about heavy metal culture and music to put the respondents at ease and help build rapport and increase the validity of the methodology.

Analysis of our findings was conducted on the basis of thematic coding strategies (Babbie 2010, p. 400). Coding occurred in various stages, first (inductively) pulling out the themes in the responses relevant to our research questions, then focusing on the women's and men's responses, respectively, and subsequently comparing them with one another. Finally, we grouped the themes into logically divided categories irrespective of the moments when they were addressed during the interviews, and we subsequently (deductively) reexamined all interviews on the basis of the discovered themes. We also explored any deviating statements made by the respondents, which were useful to understand certain areas in the heavy metal subculture on which opinions are ambivalent or more nuanced. Such deviating statements are also useful to consider in order to highlight areas that can be useful to formulate ideas for future research.

In the following chapters, we will present the findings of the interviews by providing an exposition of the themes that emerged from the data analysis. Eight themes were discovered upon various rounds of thematic coding. As mentioned, these themes reflect respondents' own understanding of self and others and should not necessarily be understood as accurate statements of fact, an issue that will be separately discussed in Chapter 8. We will explain the themes under four headings, first focusing on issues that are more generally applicable (to the entire heavy metal subculture) and subsequently centering on themes that are related to gender, with separate attention to moshing and flashing. In line with our attention to insiders' perceptions, these themes were derived from the participants' discussions of their own experiences in the heavy metal subculture and how they attach meaning to these experiences.

Reporting the study results, respondents will be identified with gender-specific names that were selected on the basis of a random name generator available online. We thus maintain our study participants' anonymity, but do indicate their gender. We will also be explicit about the central variable of gender when need be. All quoted interviews (appearing between double quotation marks) contain the precise wording used by the respondents so as not to potentially change the meaning or intent of their answers. The one respondent (Kathy) who did not allow her phone interview to be recorded is paraphrased as precisely as possible on the basis of the interviewer's notes. Quotes from interviews provided in writing are copied verbatim, including typos and misspelled words.

Chapter 5

METALHEAD: MUSIC AS IDENTITY

Turning to the first set of empirical results from the interviews, this chapter explores the self-ascribed status of the heavy metal fan as involving an all-encompassing identity and lifestyle. This finding pertains to the broadest themes revealed by the research data inasmuch as the study participants apply these characteristics to themselves and to other fans in the heavy metal sub-culture, regardless of gender or any other differentiating categories. As such, these data reveal the extent and manner in which being a fan of heavy metal, the music, and the subculture involves an overall lifestyle and identity. In the interviews, two such broad themes emerged: (1) being a metalhead is a pas-sion; and (2) a sharp distinction is drawn between the insiders of the heavy metal subculture and its outsiders.

The Metal Self

Theme 1: Heavy metal is a passion. Interview respondents often used the word "passion" to describe their participation in the heavy metal community. Using such a strongly emotional term demonstrates that being a metalhead is, to the fans of the musical genre, an important part of their overall identity, not just a matter of a musical preference. Being a metalhead is "a big part of who I am," as William stated, and involves, in Steve's words, an "emotional connection to the music." It was especially striking that the word passion was repeatedly used in response to a wide variety of interview questions, both by men and women participants alike.

When asked to describe the heavy metal community in general terms and what it means to be a ("real") metal fan, the interviews showed that it was treated as a given by most all respondents that being a fan of heavy metal revolved around "the music," "the sound," "loud, distorted guitar," and "the show," as several respondents stated plainly. But it was telling that many parti-cipants explicitly spoke of this enjoyment of music in terms of a passion. For example, Susan and Robert described metal fans in almost identical terms as, respectively, "passionate about their music" and "passionate about your

views." Pam in her response to the same question about the general characteristics of metal fans said, "You have to truly listen to the music and understand
the passion that comes with the music and understand the meaning of songs."
Later in her interview, she reiterated that as a fan of heavy metal you will be
accepted into the group if you can "show your passion is real." A lack of passion and authenticity will conversely be seen as disqualifying to subcultural
belonging. As Nicole said, "I've seen kids who run around in band shirts they
don't even listen to because they think it's 'cool.'"

Other respondents confirmed the centrality of the passion metal fans share.
Victor took a pause before answering the question to describe metal fans and
then said it was first and foremost about "passion" and that you have to be "in
it for the music, not just the image," before going on to describe his personal
interest in the music. The most striking part of his response was the clearly
deliberate and conscious decision to say the word passion, with emphasis, after
thinking about the question for a little while in order to capture the essence
of the metalhead identity. Similarly, respondent Earl stated, "I think you have
a passion for the genrera [sic] of music is the true meaning of a Metal Fan."
When asked what the characteristics of a metal fan are, Christopher kept his
response short and simple, saying, "passion for the music; not much more than
that. No need for ear gauges."

Interestingly, the significance of passion in the heavy metal identity was
also brought up in response to questions that specifically targeted if and how
gender might impact one's acceptance into the metal community, especially
for women. For instance, Pam, who commented that gender had not greatly
affected her acceptance in the metal community, stated that as a woman "your
[sic] accepted based on passion," adding that a woman who moshes "shows
her true passion." So while the word passion was used mostly in response to
questions that regarded the heavy metal subculture as a whole, it also came up
again in regard to women acceptance more in particular.

Us and Them

**Theme 2: A sharp distinction exists between insiders and out-
siders.** Respondents often stated that they see and make a clear separation
between those who belong to the heavy metal community and those who do
not and, relatedly, that insiders' perspectives of the heavy metal subculture
differ greatly from outsiders' perspectives. As with the theme of passion, the in-
sider/outsider theme was prevalent among both men and women in our study.

Most participants in our research recognized that there exists a relatively
uniform negative stereotype of what a heavy metal fan is in the broader society outside of the subculture. But realizing the objective existence of said

stereotype among metalheads does not, of course, mean it is accepted as valid within the metal community. For although heavy metal fans, in William's words, "don't really care what society thinks about them," the respondents commented in very deliberate terms that they do not conform to the stereotype others have of them and that the subculture actually includes a lot of diversity. Interestingly, the comments that were made on diversity generally pertained more to diversity among men in the heavy metal community, not diversity with respect to gender, race, or sexual orientation.

Many participants commented on the outsider's stereotype of metal fans, and some expressed the opinion that fans conforming to this stereotype do exist but are not reflective of what all, or even the majority, of metal fans are actually like. For example, Peter explained at some length,

> LOL I understand there is a definite stereotype of the long haired guy with his leather jacket, sub-primate IQ, and 400 tattoos, but honestly I think the only universal characteristic of metal fans is the love of the heavily distorted guitar. I think we'd all like to think that heavy metal fans MUST have some inner sense of rebellion, but the truth is you'll find your share of guys and gals who would proudly identify themselves as conservative Republicans at any rock concert in any genre of music. Hell, my in laws are the biggest Republicans that I've ever met and they gave me a Metallica beanie for Christmas last year.

Respondent Kelly agreed that the outsiders' perspective of metalheads is "not a good stereotype" of kids who are "not in college... on drugs... drinking... have gauges, dreads, black hair, piercings... all black clothing." A similar sentiment that relates the stereotype of the metalhead primarily to intelligence, or rather an assumed lack thereof, was implicitly acknowledged by Paula who realized that outsiders think of metal fans as "guys in leather" with "low IQ" and "many tats." Likewise, Nick argued in direct opposition to this outsiders' viewpoint, "I think metal fans are generally intelligent, thoughtful people." The adoption of a standardized fashion and style among metalheads was recognized by Steve, who said that "there certainly seems to be a uniform for attending shows that consists of jeans, t shirt, and piercings."

Yet, although some respondents think that a uniform stereotype of their subculture exists, they disagree rather strongly with its validity. Both men and women metal fans concur on this matter. By example, Frances argued, "Honestly there is no set 'type' of a fan. I've known very respectable people in the community to love metal, as well as the stereotype." She went on to describe metalheads, deliberately against the stereotypical judgments outsiders are thought to have, as "less judgmental than most people, [...] very kind, and honest people. Fun, and some even quirky." Similarly, respondents Steve, Susan, and Peter described metalheads as "more accepting," "very loyal," and "the most loyal fan base in the world." Respondent Nick spoke of them as "intelligent, well spoken" even when they "see themselves as weirdos and out-casts." He continued, "I don't think one could stereotype metal fans as far as their outward appearance goes as many fans of metal look no different than any other segment of society."

It is interesting to note that, to describe their own community of metalheads, the study participants frequently spoke about what outsiders think, even though and when they were not asked to do so. This explicit mentioning of others thereby shows that the differentiation between insiders ("us") and out-siders ("them") is of considerable importance to the fans in identifying and presenting their music subculture. For example, Paula said she thought fans of heavy metal "are misunderstood. Society thinks of the metal fan base as hood-lums, trashy, etc." Paraphrasing the words of Kathy (who declined her phone interview to be recorded), she gave a similar response, stating that "the group is intimidating to outsiders, who do not understand the music" and wrongly assume metalheads "don't work, don't have real jobs."

Respondent Janice gave her opinion on the characteristics of the heavy metal community explicitly in terms of a dichotomy between insiders and outsiders. Whereas, she said, outsiders view the metal subculture as charac-terized by "long hair, black clothing, dirty, wearing denim vests, patches and male," insiders realize there is much greater diversity in terms of "are all sorts of demographics, males, women, some look like they don't belong at all. It's not about what you wear or how you look to be a Metal fan." Paula similarly referred to "outsiders" and the "stereotype" they have about heavy metal, spe-cifically mentioning the example of how metal fans are assumed to dress when she as a metalhead, in fact, dresses "normal most of the time."

Respondents made several statements about the diversity they see among metalheads. Strikingly, however, they would usually give examples that per-tained to the men in heavy metal. The instance that was mentioned most often in this respect, seeking to counter the outsider's stereotype of the typical metalhead, was of the man who shows up to a metal show dressed in a suit and tie. For example, Catherine said, "It all depends on the person. Generally metal fans can be easily recognized by their look. But the look is not every-thing. You could be facing someone wearing a suit without even knowing that he absolutely loves metal." Similarly referencing men's style of dress, Nicole said, "I've seen people who dress in nothing but suits and ties and love Slayer."

In sum, the general themes of the heavy metal identity discussed in this chapter show that the participants of our study view their subculture as a passionate community of metalheads that distinguishes itself from the mainstream society of outsiders. Indicating the strong identity and sense of self of the metalhead, it is striking to note that the study participants would often answer general questions to describe the metal fan and the metal community with explicit reference to what they claim outsiders might think of them. Though formulated in nonsuggestive ways, the very question to define and describe heavy metal fans and their subculture, in other words, invokes by its members a strong sense of self that is especially articulated in relation to others. Revealing a measure of defensiveness, a need is expressed to justify oneself and the subculture against an external stereotype that, metalheads believe, is how they are labeled and accordingly treated.

Most of the information given by the study participants concerning the passion and us-versus-them dichotomy of the metalhead identity was provided, not surprisingly, during the first few questions of the interviews that pertained to the heavy metal subculture in general. However, as the sequence of the interview questions was purposefully designed to see if and how gender would also be brought up when these broader questions were asked, it is striking that we found that most respondents while talking about these general matters used pronouns and physical descriptions of fans who were men. Only later during the interviews, when questions were asked specifically about gender, would participants typically begin to differentiate men and women within the heavy metal community and then, ironically, most often proclaim that the subculture is marked by equality with respect to gender.

Chapter 6

METAL WOMAN: BEING AND PLAYING GENDER

The central sociological focus on gender in the heavy metal subculture was in the interviews addressed by means of questions concerning the position of women metalheads and the masculinity of the culture. Yet, we were also able to rely on less direct ways to estimate the significance of gender by identifying and differentiating men and women among the respondents to see how their gender might affect certain otherwise non–gender-related answers. Additionally, separate attention was devoted to asking questions about moshing and flashing as two relatively common practices at (some) heavy metal shows that are forms of fan conduct with obvious gender connotations. How do metalheads perceive of these practices today as women are increasingly taking up more equal roles in the heavy metal culture? This chapter will show what role, according to metalheads themselves, the issue of gender in heavy metal plays today, and if women do, can, and/or should mosh (as the men of metal do) and whether they do, can, and ought to flash (for the pleasure of men).

Being Woman in Heavy Metal

Two central themes emerged in the interviews with both men and women respondents with respect to the relevance of gender and the status of women in heavy metal: (1) there is a special need as a woman in heavy metal to prove oneself; and (2) women metalheads, more than men, have to rely on physical markers or symbols to emphasize that they too are fans of the genre and belong to the subculture.

Theme 3: Women in heavy metal face a special need to prove themselves. The theme of women metalheads having to prove themselves as members of the heavy metal community jumped out from the interviews as among the most prevalent findings of our study. This finding readily conforms to our perspective of heavy metal as a homosocial environment that is dominated by men. But it is additionally noteworthy to observe that the interview respondents, both the women and the men, are themselves also aware of this gender issue. Explicitly asked if the metal scene was dominated by men and hypermasculine in nature, almost all participants unequivocally answered in the affirmative. Sometimes, the homosocial character of heavy metal was implied, such as when Victor said he would "like to see more females." And at least one respondent, Susan, described the heavy metal subculture as made up of "mostly males" even when she was only asked to provide a general description.

In view of heavy metal's generally acknowledged hypermasculinity, the majority of women participants in the interviews felt that they needed to do some form of "proving" in order to be accepted into the group. For example, Kelly said that as a woman in heavy metal, "you have to know what you're talking about, know the bands." Pam similarly stated that a woman in metal will be accepted "if you can prove your [sic] not just listening to be cool." The most distinct requirement on the part of women metalheads to demonstrate that they deserve to belong and be accepted in the metal community relates to having an expert knowledge of the musical genre. As Kathy argued, as a woman "you gotta know the bands." Even when one's gender was not seen as relevant, respondents realize that it might matter to others and hence, paradoxically, was relevant nonetheless. Asked if her gender mattered in being accepted in metal, Nicole stated, "Personally I could give a fuck what others think of me. That's their problem, not mine."

The most detailed responses on the subject of women metalheads needing to prove themselves came from respondents Sarah and Nicole. "Our intentions are doubted until we 'prove' ourselves worthy," Sarah stated. She continued, "I'm occasionally asked where my boyfriend is, supposedly under the assumption that I wouldn't be at a heavy metal show out of my own interest. In fact, many of us have to show a masculine side to be more accepted by some... Though having to prove that every time gets very tedious after a while." Nicole likewise argued that "some girls are there to make gaga eyes at the band members but a lot of them are there for the music. Too bad closed-minded guys don't see it that way. You have to somehow prove your worth and all that crap." There was wide consensus among the women respondents on this issue.

Unlike the experiences from the interviewed women, almost all men in our study argued that just going to metal shows alone was enough for them (as men) to be accepted into the group. At best, the style of dress was thought to be somewhat relevant. "For a man to be accepted," said Steve, he would "probably only need to show up in a black t-shirt and [have] rudimentary knowledge of the band's music." Similarly, Peter said about attending his first metal show in the 1980s,

I wore my football jersey and nice jeans because it was on a school night and we had had football practice that day. As excited as I was to be going to my first metal show, I couldn't help but feel that something was amiss. Finally I realized that I was the only person in attendance that wasn't wearing a black t-shirt and ripped jeans.

But, even as Peter pointed out the need for proper heavy metal attire, he did not define style of dress in terms of having to prove himself as a metal fan; only that the experience was an issue he had personally experienced, not necessarily reflective of his identify as a man among men. In fact, at his next concert, he was amused to say, he purposely "wore a WHITE Amy Grant t-shirt (borrowed from a cousin, I despise Gospel music) and khaki pants. [...] My friends didn't want to sit with me, but I had a point to prove."

In the context of being accepted as a fan, Tom brought up an issue that was otherwise not targeted in the study, namely the fact that he, as a Korean American, argued that ethnicity and race also matter. In fact, Tom explicitly said during the interview that our research, with its interest in differences and inequalities, should focus on all minorities in the metal subculture, not just the women. As a member of an ethnic minority, Tom spoke of having to prove himself extra to be accepted in the heavy metal community in a manner formally similar to the experience of women. To be accepted alongside the other metal fans, he said,

see, for me it's acknowledging a lot of the classics like um you have to acknowledge the importance of bands like Anthrax, Iron Maiden, Motorhead, or Black Sabbath uh and I guess like the old school bands like death metal like Slayer, Metallica, so then there's that acceptance as long as you acknowledge that those bands are important that is acceptance.

Our study did not contain an ethnically or otherwise diverse group of respondents (besides the two selected gender categories), but some participants brought up differences and inequities in the metal community other than those based on gender. In her description of the metal scene as comprising mostly men, for instance, Susan further described metalheads as "blue-collar workers," the one time when class was explicitly brought up during the interviews. At least one additional principle of stratification was discovered during the interviews when Robert revealed the relevance of his sexual orientation. "As a gay man," he said, "I've not always felt really welcome in the community. That's a shame, isn't it? It doesn't have anything to do with the music and the music is what unites us." Catherine was the only other respondent who brought up sexual orientation when she mentioned that she had "even attended several metal concerts with gay and transgender people." As with ethnicity and class, sexual orientation was otherwise not specifically addressed in our interviews, but it is clear that the issue of minority representation in heavy metal does not only revolve around gender.

Lines of separation and stratification in the heavy metal subculture are also made, so our interviews revealed, on the basis of expertise (and its association with age) of the musical style itself as well as its various (sub)genres. As Tom stated, "I hear a lot from the elitist point of view or old school guys." Similarly discussing the topic, Timothy admitted of metalheads, "Some can be almost elitist." Nicole even expressed disapproval of "the term 'real metal fan,'" which she said "smacks of elitism and that's not what Metal is all about." In general, it is likely that minority members in the metal subculture (including racial minorities, younger, or older fans depending on the genre) feel a special need to prove themselves as true experts of metal, whereas, as our study shows, white men think you just need to go to metal shows to be in and of the heavy metal community.

Theme 4: Women need to rely on physical markers and symbols to affirm their identity as metalheads. One way for women to prove themselves as legit metalheads is to literally show their allegiance and identity by means of dress and in other visible and tangible ways. While this theme was not discovered among the majority of women interviewed, it was more common for the women to discuss having to buy merchandise to establish their metalhead identity than it was for the men. Even when no explicit reference is made to gender, it is striking that men considerably less feel the need to discuss such observable attributes in practicing the metal lifestyle.

Several women among the respondents spoke about the importance of buying heavy metal merchandise items and clothing, especially second-hand T-shirts. For example, Sarah said, "heavy metal [...] seeps into multiple facets of their life, whether that includes moshing at concerts, collecting rare vinyl of obscure metal bands or just listening to hours of metal in their free time." Janice agreed that buying merchandise like band T-shirts was important to be seen as a metalhead, consequently attributing her identity of self to the perception of others. Pam brought the same need for physical markers up several times in her interview with statements like "Support them by buying there [sic] CDs and apparell [sic]" and "Don't wear the shirt if you don't know the band."

In sum, women metalheads express a special need to prove themselves as valid and valued members of the heavy metal community, especially in terms of their expertise and knowledge of the music and its performers. An additional such special need was expressed by the ethnic minority man among the respondents of our study and may, as such, reveal a more general characteristic of all metalheads who have a minority status, whether it be based on gender, race, ethnicity, sexual orientation, age, and other differentiating variables. The related theme of the need to rely on physical markers to be accepted as a metalhead that was revealed in the interviews has relevance from a gender perspective inasmuch as no men discussed buying things as part of their experience in the subculture. Based on the broader statements about the metal identity expressed by the women respondents, this theme can be argued to imply that women metal fans feel a special need for physical markers, more than men do, to show they are fans of the genre as another way of having to prove themselves.

Playing Gender: Between Moshing and Flashing

Moshing and flashing are two specific acts in rock and metal we expressly investigated in the interviews because of their obvious gender relevance. Moshing is a relatively violent form of dancing thought of as masculine, whereas flashing is a sexually explicit practice only women can engage in. Exploring how moshing and flashing might affect women's status in the heavy metal community, two themes emerged from the interviews: (1) women in heavy metal who take part in moshing receive more respect; and (2) flashing leads to defensive othering.

Theme 5: Women metalheads who participate in moshing receive more respect. The theme that women metalheads taking part in moshing receive more respect was revealed from the interviews with both women and men. Respondents thereby mentioned the relevance of a moshing woman's physical size, which for women was interpreted as a matter of defensive othering, while the men discussed it from the viewpoint of concerns over safety and harm.

Performing the conventionally understood to be more masculine act of moshing was generally seen among the respondents to add to the amount of respect a woman received from her fellow metalheads. For example, Pam commented that a woman who moshes is "brave definitely" and that any injuries only result "because of the excitement." Kathy said that a woman moshing "earns respect from the guys for sure," while Susan commented, "It may actually show that she can 'hang' with the guys." In these statements, then, we see how women moshing connects with respect explicitly in connection with men and the notion, as Timothy said, that metal is distinctly "hypermasculine in the pit."

Several of the women interviewed said they did not engage in moshing, even though their sentiments about moshing were not necessarily negative. For example, Nicole said, "I don't mosh, but I've had my nose broken by kids who flail around and don't watch where they're going." Kathy said she stayed "away from" moshing, but (possibly because) she was once "sucked in [a mosh pit] while pregnant." Paula likewise had never been in a mosh pit and thought of it as something "dangerous" and more suited for men. Frances similarly found moshing to be "quite physical" and did not involve with it as it seemed "senseless" to her. She laughed when asked if moshing would give women in heavy metal more respect, stating "I have no idea. LOL."

The men interviewed for this study tended to agree that women in heavy metal will earn respect by participating in mosh pits. Timothy, for instance, stated that a woman moshing "gives her a better reputation. Newer people in the group find them more 'hardcore' than others." Earl agreed with the sentiment, though he expressed his feelings only after being prompted by the interviewer. Initially saying he was "not really sure," he was asked to give his own personal thoughts when he saw a woman mosh, upon which he said: "In my opinion if the woman is moshes [*sic*] it means she is definately [*sic*] hardcore and a fan of the band. It also shows she can keep her own and hang with the guys. I would think she would be more accepted more into the heavy metal subculture group." So again, a woman moshing is thought of as earning respect, but on terms related to her association with men. For that reason also, as Nick stated, women who mosh are safe because the "guys will protect her."

Two statements in the interviews concerning moshing stood out as instances of defensive othering, indicating women metalheads to aspire to masculinity by distancing themselves from other women. Kelly said about women moshers, "They are looked up to [...] it's about taking turns." She then went on to tell a story about a time when she thought of a woman moshing as harmful because it involved a "fat chick" who, she thought, might cause people to get hurt. Resorting to a rather traditional gender norm concerning a woman's expected weight, she made no comparable mention about the size of men moshing, although they can reasonably be assumed to be physically larger and more readily capable of causing harm. Also suggesting defensive othering, Sarah said that sometimes

> there are women who don't understand the proper way to mosh in different scenarios. I've seen women try too hard to fit in and try to mosh but just get hurt and embarrass themselves. I've also seen women initiate

mosh pits and go in harder than some of the men. If she shows she knows what she's doing, thus displaying masculine qualities, she is further accepted into the group.

This quote is very descriptive and literally comments on how masculine qualities raise a woman's status in the heavy metal subculture, supporting the notion of defensive othering because special value is placed on women who act like men.

When the men who were interviewed for this study mentioned the physical characteristics and body size of women moshers, which they occasionally did, they always did so based on their masculine ideas of women's femininity and a woman's position as being more vulnerable and in need of protection. By example, Nick said that "a smaller girl might get protection," referring to the men besides her having to mosh differently. "At a mosh pit," Robert argued, "everybody should be aware of what they're doing, no matter the gender. And when a girl is moshing against a guy, then the guy needs to be aware of her physical status." The statement is paradoxical, if not outright internally contradictory, by arguing that gender does (or should) not matter but also does matter, specifically in terms of the size of the body moshing, though only when it concerns a woman because it is assumed she is in need of protection.

The rather conventional masculine emphasis in discussions about moshing on women's safety is not unrelated to some of the issues some women respondents brought up in relation to danger and physicality. But unlike the women who did not mosh because of safety concerns many men will also share (as most fans at metal shows do not participate in moshing), the men interviewed in our study discussed a moshing woman's safety in distinctly gendered terms only applicable to her and other women. At the same time, these men may have been overlooking concrete situations of physical harm women can face when they are caught in a mosh. Kathy's involuntary involvement in a mosh pit while she was pregnant is a striking example.

In terms of the masculine qualities attributed to moshing, some of the men interviewed ironically used strongly gendered language when commenting on women metalheads who mosh. For example, Christopher commented about a woman moshing, "That is a ballsy move, but good for her." Tom likewise said a woman moshing "is cool [...] if she had the balls to do it." The use of the words "ballsy" and "balls" evidently identifies the act of moshing as a masculine behavior, one which can earn women who do it respect. Additionally revealing a gendered dimension, Christopher said about women moshing that he was "sure it is accepted amongst the true moshers." The "true" moshers are implicitly all men.

Theme 6: Flashing is responded to by means of defensive othering.
The women interviewed in this study generally view the act of flashing in negative terms and distance themselves from the women who engage in the practice. For example, Janice said that flashing gives a woman a "groupie status," while Sarah agreed, "Depending on who you ask, she might not be taken as seriously as a metal fan, and it might be assumed that she's looking to hook up with someone rather than to enjoy the music." Both quotes are condemnations of flashing as an act profoundly unmetal and unworthy of metalheads, because it is thought to have nothing to do with enjoying the music but instead redefines the woman as seeking sexual attention.

There is broad consensus among the women interviewed for our study concerning the negative attitude toward flashing in the heavy metal community. For example, Susan said about a woman flashing, "It may show she's not as into the music as others, or she just wants attention." Frances, as another example of defensive othering, clarified her position explicitly as "a woman," implicitly recognizing that men might see this differently. She clarified, "I guess because I'm a woman I just think it's senseless, and view it as someone trying to get some attention. Usually it's just accepted as 'it's going to happen' at any concert."

As indicated by the quoted interviews, the questions on flashing (as on moshing) solicited a lot of responses whereby women would clearly indicate that these were their own personal views, as indicated by their use of a lot of "I" statements rather than responding in terms of how the larger subculture would view these issues (as they did for other questions). For example, Paula commented about flashing, "I personally think it's trashy but it's part of the culture." Likewise, Catherine said, "I never encountered a woman in my group who did such a thing during a concert." Defensive othering is present because the women discussing flashing in their interviews differentiate and distance themselves as individuals ("I") from other women ("them") who engage in an act they view as negative for all women ("us").

It is worth noting that the women metalheads participating in this study who did not portray the act of flashing in a negative way would typically laugh when responding to interview questions about it. The phone interview with Kathy, for instance, had a friendly but otherwise serious tone until the question of flashing came up. Asked about the why of a woman metalhead flashing, she began laughing, took a pause, and said, "I guess she's having a good time," before trailing off and laughing again. In her online interview, Pam said that women who flash are "more confident, badass Lol crazy," one of only two times the respondent wrote "lol." The fact that the only women in our study who did not speak of flashing in an expressly negative way still found the thought of it humorous could show that flashing is something that might be made fun of by other women.

The men participating in this study gave mixed answers on the question of flashing. Some men clearly expressed they viewed flashing in a negative way. For example, Christopher said, "I can only speak for myself, but I wouldn't say I gain respect for them when they do." William likewise stated,

> Honestly, I have always found myself to be very embarrassed for the women who do that. Some may do it to get the attention of band members, but I have been able to do that just with screaming along, throwing the horns, etc. I never got the concept of a woman pulling up her shirt to get a bunch of sweaty guys to freak out. I would never outwardly shame them […] it's just something I never really got.

Making these statements on flashing, the quoted men were elaborate in their explanations and used personal "I" statements as did the women who also viewed the act negatively, indicating a consensus among these respondents to distance themselves from women who flash.

Other men interviewed in our study gave relatively neutral or evasive responses that did not really indicate whether they saw it as positive or negative to women metalheads and the scene in general. Though generally distancing themselves from flashing, they saw it as something they were "not sure" about (Timothy) and thought it was "not common" (Victor), something that happened "more in rock shows" (Tom), or "just something that some people do" (Steve). Earl was the sole participant who commented on flashing in a more approving manner. Although he was initially hesitant as "not really sure" before being probed to answer the question about women moshing, he was quick to respond to the question about flashing, stating, "The guys love it! It certainly brings her A LOT OF ATTENTION!!! LOL." Strikingly, the respondent thus spoke of "the guys" rather than using an "I" statement to denote his own option. The respondent's less personalized statement could have been influenced by the fact that the interviewer is a woman.

Similar to how men in our study view of women metalheads who engage in moshing in terms of safety concerns, one respondent brought up the possibility of sexual assault in connection with flashing. Nick, in particular, said that flashing "doesn't end well […] [and] can be seen as an invitation to get frisky. You hear about it leading to sexual assault." He went on to give a detailed example of an incident at a live show of thrash metal band Exodus, where a woman who was crowd-surfing took her shirt off and was groped the whole time while she was surfing. When her boyfriend tried to approach some of the guys who were inappropriately touching her, both he and his girlfriend ended up being kicked out of the show (while the gropers were allowed to stay), illustrating a clear case of victim blaming in sexual assaults.

Summing up, this chapter has shown that along with the finding that women in heavy metal feel a need to prove themselves beyond what the men need to do and rely on physical markers more than they think men have to do, the gendered acts of moshing and flashing are interpreted accordingly. A woman moshing is seen as a sign that she belongs, and is actively seeking to be accepted, in the heavy metal community. At the same time, the expressed perceptions on women moshing are also revealing of the fact that a woman's identity and membership in heavy metal can only be determined in terms set by men. An assumed vulnerability and the need to protect moshing women from potential harm additionally reflect this masculine understanding.

Flashing is widely mocked and condemned among the metalheads we interviewed as something that is silly or even inappropriate and a potentially dangerous kind of sexualized behavior. This opinion may be reflective of changes that have taken place in the heavy metal scene, especially the move from commercial heavy metal in the 1980s to the various underground and so-called extreme forms of today that are considered more authentically metal. Also playing a part may have been the growing and more active roles that women in heavy metal wish to play today. These variations and changes in the world of heavy metal are discussed in the next chapter.

Chapter 7

DEGREES OF METAL: VARIATION AND CHANGE

The respondents in our study agree that there are more women today taking up more diverse positions and roles in the world of heavy metal than before. This perception is as clear as much as its consequences, meaning, and future directions remain as yet uncertain. The final empirical dimension of the interview findings relates to the fact that heavy metal fans understand that, in terms of gender and other issues, there are important variations and dimensions of continuity and change in the heavy metal subculture. This finding is not surprising given the fact that heavy metal has been around for several decades and has seen trends and fashions come and go, along with demographic and other changes, while nonetheless still identifiable as a particular form of popular music culture. With respect to these differences, the following two final themes emerged from the interview data: (1) metal fans perceive that there are more and less important differences in terms of gender across the various subgenres of heavy metal; and (2) they also argue that the conditions of the heavy metal subculture are generally changing in a positive direction for women. Both men and women interviewed in our study acknowledge these variations across metal's genres and its changes over time.

Styles of Heavy Metal

Theme 7: Important differences exist across subgenres in heavy metal. The theme of consequential differences existing across metal's different subgenres (beyond their musical aspects) emerged frequently during the interviews. These differences were raised, not so much in the questions asking to address gender issues, as in the general questions about the heavy metal community. Many participants found the general questions about heavy metal and its fans hard to answer because, they said, it depended on the specific (sub) genre of heavy metal music and its associated fans and their scene. While respondents recognized a relatively uniform stereotype of the metalhead among the community's outsiders, they were quick to add that insiders are aware of the differences and disagreements among the many metalheads across various subgenres. For example, Timothy argued that a fan being accepted in heavy metal depends on the subgenre they are trying to belong to. "Depends on the group," he said when asked about the acceptance of women in heavy metal, explaining, "Most would need to listen to the same genre of metal. Especially when you get into the more extreme genres. It also helps to be friends with someone in the group or know someone in the group." Similarly, Robert said, "I've seen all kinds of metal fans, as well as I've seen all kinds of people in each subcultural group."

Some respondents discussed how they feel that heavy metal is too much fragmented into too many different subgenres and that some fans are elitist about their favorite subgenre. For example, Peter complained that "metal has become fractured into a hundred different sub genres [sic] nowadays, which is annoying as hell when your only concern is 'Is the song good or not?'" Tom spoke of the elitism he found to exist across certain subgenres, especially dividing the older and the more recent styles of heavy metal. Referencing so-called metalcore groups, a relatively recent genre whose fans tend to be as young as high school age and which older metalheads sometimes disparage as not "really" heavy metal, he said that especially the "old schoolers or elitists" have a "hate" and throw "accusations [...] towards the core bands a lot."

Women participants expressed similar thoughts about the differences that exist across heavy metal's many subgenres and, more noticeably so than the men, expressed these variations also in terms of gender-related issues, such as moshing and flashing. "Interactions between metal fans at shows often varies by the subgenre," commented metalhead Sarah, specifically suggesting that "heavier types like thrash, death, and grindcore often include mosh pits in the middle of the floor. Other genres like progressive, slower types of black metal and classic heavy metal usually don't, so fans usually stand still or headbang with others when appropriate."

Likewise relating to the relevance of heavy metal's subgenres, the general consensus among the respondents of our study is that flashing is not really part of the contemporary styles of the heavy metal scene, but mostly a thing of the older and more commercially oriented hair bands and glam genres of metal. Paula expressed this idea well, arguing "I haven't seen [flashing] as much in metal than I have at 80s hair band concerts (Motley Crue, Poison, etc.)." Similarly, Kelly commented that flashing "only happened at more rock concerts [...] the pretty tame metal," and Catherine said she had "never encountered a woman in my group who did such thing during a concert." Nicole likewise wondered about flashing, "People actually still do that at metal gigs? I don't know what Metal gigs you go to, but they don't happen at mine. I haven't seen someone flash since Poison in the 80s and 90s." Indicating the relevance of changes that have taken place, respondents argue that flashing is not as common as it used to be and that, conversely, women in the contemporary metal scene wish to be treated on more equal terms.

Heavy Metal History

Theme 8: The heavy metal subculture is changing in a positive direction in terms of the inclusion and acceptance of women. While some of our study participants, especially the women, spoke about how the metal subculture is still more challenging for women members, the majority of respondents stated that the situation has been changing for the better over the years. Whether this is an accurate reflection of the realities women in heavy metal are confronted with and are experiencing today is, of course, another matter, but it accurately reflects respondents' self-understanding.

For example, Frances stated, "More and more women are around and bands, too, every year." As a result, metal's hypermasculinity is "starting to go away [...] before yeah it definitely was like 80s thrash was male dominated [...] today there are more women lead singers," Janice said, and relatedly, she argued that flashing is therefore also not as common anymore. "More women are taking charge in the genre," commented Sarah, who made special mention of the diverse presence of women in the metal world: "There are women metal journalists, photographers and concert promoters as well. I'm a singer in a heavy metal band myself [...] most people will listen to my music and see me for who I am and not my gender." As these quotes indicate, special meaning is assigned to the presence of women as lead singers and other performers in some of the newer genres of metal and how this integration among performers is seen as a sign of positive change that has also affected metal's fanbase.

Other respondents, including the men, reiterated the observation that women are more present in today's metal scene. "The older I get," argued William, "the more evidence I see of women metal fans, which I think is awesome." The oldest metal fan interviewed in this study, William, went on to say that the once more difficult acceptance of women in heavy metal "is a thing of the past now. I think it is fantastic to see women, especially women of all ages, at shows." Similarly, Timothy said,

When I first became a fan it was way harder for a woman to be accepted. I've seen that shift over the years. [...] Everything about women has changed since I first became a fan. They used to be the "holders" of things at shows. The watchers of drinks. Now everything has changed. It's weird now if I go to a show and not see a female in the pit.

Robert confirmed the sentiment, stating, "Things have been changing these past years with more and more female-fronted bands becoming successful. And that's great because we need more diversity. We need more diversity in our music. And we need more diversity in our cultural views."

In spite of the acknowledged advances women metalheads have made, it is also understood, by at least a number of interview respondents, that women fans still face obstacles being accepted into the heavy metal community. Kathy, for example, thought that even in today's heavy metal culture "girls are supposed to do girly stuff" and that at least some of the men "don't think we can be hardcore." The most elaborate statements and strongest opinions on the relevance of gender came again from Nicole and Sarah, clearly the most outspoken participants in our study. Nicole complained that her "only gripe [...] is the whole attitude against female fans. Some guys seem to think that female fans are only there to stare at the band members. [...] I grew past that obsession back in high school. Now it's the music that gets my attention." Herself a heavy metal musician, Sarah agreed, "My gender does affect my acceptance into the group of heavy metal fans," adding that "females are often doubted as being 'real metal fans.'"

Despite the general idea that the conditions for women in heavy metal are thought to have improved over the years, some men in the interviews also acknowledged that it might still be harder for a woman to be a metalhead. For example, Steve said, "For a woman to be accepted she would probably be called upon to have a much more extensive knowledge of the band and the genre before being accepted as a true fan." Tom, who faced his own issues of acceptance as a Korean, commented that women in heavy metal today still "receive fire from both sides, guys and girls" inasmuch as "guys probably think you're like the cool girl and the girls probably think you're like the crazy chick (laughing)." Moreover, Tom added, "society thinks it worse for females to be metal fans" and "metal would do it too, but not as bad as society."

In sum, our study shows that fans of heavy metal today are generally well aware of the relevance of gender as an important aspect of their community. As the respondents in our interviews reveal, metalheads recognize the relevance of these gendered conditions especially in view of heavy metal's longstanding tradition of men being dominantly present and hypermasculinity being a traditional aspect of its culture. At the same time, women are acknowledged to have taken on roles of more diverse kinds in today's heavy metal subculture, albeit in varying degrees across the music' subgenres and their respective communities. Yet, while positive changes are recognized among fans to have taken place for women to be better represented in heavy metal, the overall situation today is still essentially seen as one marked by ambiguity. This finding is most poignantly brought out in our research by the fact that women metalheads acknowledge the remaining difficulties for their acceptance in the subculture better than the men do. This ambiguity that characterizes the contemporary situation of the gender question in heavy metal leads us to discuss, in the next chapter, the development of feminism in the subculture.

Chapter 8

TOWARD HEAVY METAL FEMINISM?

We didn't choose the easy path, but we are still standing. Carrying the torch of the women who dared before us. Never giving up when it felt like we had nothing left to give. Proving time and time again that we can fight through it and come out alive.

Alecia "Mixi" Demner, lead singer of Stitched Up Heart
(Stitched Up Heart 2018)

A study of fan perceptions of the gender dynamics in the traditionally homosocial and hypermasculine environment of the heavy metal subculture, this work was sociologically framed on the basis of gender difference theories, specifically centered on salient gender phenomena involving othering/gender performativity, objectification, and doing gender. The empirical research was specifically aimed at developing an interpretive understanding of attitudes about gender expressed by women and men who self-identify as metalheads. Relying on semi-structured interviews, we thereby sought to uncover the meanings metalheads themselves attach to the conditions and development of those aspects of the heavy metal subculture that relate closely to gender. Following the famous Thomas theorem that ideas are real in their consequences (Merton 1995), perceptions are far from trivial to examine. How fans feel and think about women as members of the heavy metal community will also shape how gender dynamics will develop and evolve. Our study has thus provided important empirical data concerning how and to what extent women are accepted and treated in an environment that is still—though less clearly than in the not too distant past—dominated by men.

It was a particular goal of our work to illustrate the value of applying a sociological perspective rooted in theories of gender difference in the world of heavy metal. Restricted to examining fan perceptions on women in heavy metal on the basis of the theory of doing gender, we recognize our study's limitations in not being able to generalize from the interview findings. A large-scale quantitative survey of the heavy metal community and its many sociologically relevant dimensions still remains to be done. A complementary analysis of the conduct that men engage in at metal shows, rather than treating masculinity as a background condition, would also enrich the scholarly study of gender in heavy metal. Yet, while our research objectives are necessarily limited in terms of generalizability, the value of our research should derive from its effort to provide depth and thick description to uncover the interpretations and meanings ascribed by participants in the heavy metal community.

To conclude this book, in this final chapter we will first review the empirical results of our study on the perceived status of women in the heavy metal community in relation to the relevant findings from the existing literature. We are especially interested to see if our findings are confirmed in other research and, in turn, seek to show how our work can offer added insights, especially inasmuch as our work is explicitly framed as a study of gender rather than a study of heavy metal. We will next relate the empirical results back to the theoretical perspective and central questions upon which we relied to examine the dynamics of gender that exist in the heavy metal subculture. This questioning of gender sociologically will lead us to reflect on some of the implications and directions of these developments in terms of the possible formation of a culture of heavy metal feminism. This chapter will therefore begin with a clarification of the contemporary state of women in heavy metal, then extend the discussion to the role of gender, and, finally, address the conflicting dynamics of continued sexism, on the one hand, and developing feminism, on the other, in connection with women's growing presence in heavy metal. We end by connecting our research findings on the heavy metal community to broader patterns of gender, society, and culture.

Women

Briefly summarizing the findings of our study in terms of the five research questions we formulated at the beginning of our work, the interview respondents argued that being a metalhead centrally involves around a passion for the music and its associated elements of an encompassing lifestyle, a theme that other scholars have found to be important in the heavy metal community as well (Laaksonen et al. 2011; O'Hagan 2021a; Purcell 2015; Riches 2011). On the basis of the interview findings, the reasons expressed for joining the subculture vary, but the overarching consensus among respondents is that heavy metal fans enjoy their favorite music and the participation in its lifestyle. Many fans also feel they are different from mainstream society, a sentiment the music precisely allows them to embrace. These themes of metalheads' (subjective) sense of self and their (intersubjective) relation to the wider community in terms of an us-versus-them mentality resonate well with insights from scholarship that has focused attention on matters of identity and belonging and the juxtaposition between insiders and outsiders in the heavy metal community (Arnett 1996; Gaines 1998; Larsson 2013; Snell and Hodgetts 2007; Walser 1993; Weinstein 2000).

Turning to issues specifically related to the status of women in the heavy metal community, the participants in our study described their subculture as (still) being dominated by men and masculine in character. This finding confirms the value of our perspective to conceive of the heavy metal subculture as a homosocial environment that is traditionally characterized by a relatively high degree of hypermasculinity. At the same time, respondents also acknowledged that the presence of women in metal has increased significantly, an almost trivial finding given the widely recognized expanded (though uneven) participation of women in heavy metal today (Berkers and Schaap 2018; Overell 2012; Schaap and Berkers 2014). The specific values associated with heavy metal, in combination with a growing presence of women metalheads, harmonize with our understanding of the heavy metal community—conceptually following Miller's (1998, 2001) research on gangs—as a mixed-gender subculture.

The changed and changing presence of women in the contemporary heavy metal community need not lead us to develop a new methodology of research, as some have erroneously suggested (DiGioia and Helfrich 2018), but, rather, should make scholars more sensitive to the new realities that are presented. To be sure, as we argued before, the themes relating to participants' understanding of their identity and community cannot be taken at face value, but they are relevant to understand how metalheads perceive their subculture. And they will also have a sense of reality, however limited at times. Besides, the literature on heavy metal referenced throughout this study confirms a general increase of women participants, albeit in uneven ways and with unclear implications.

Turning to the perceived consequences of the feminization of the metal community, responses from our study's participants are revealing in several respects. The women interviewed for this study gave mixed responses to the question if they felt discriminated against by other metalheads because of their gender. Some women metalheads felt that sexism and misogynistic attitudes still have to be addressed in heavy metal, but others did not. This difference may be related to both changes over time and will also depend on variations across heavy metal's many subgenres, ranging from mainstream metal to its most obscure and underground forms (Barron 2013; Heesch and Scott 2016; Jocson-Singh 2016; Kitteringham 2014; Vasan 2010). These genre distinctions not only relate to musical differences but also pertain to social and cultural variations in the various spheres of the metal subculture (Gracyk 2016). The variations that exist among these (plural) genres do not invalidate the conception of heavy metal as a subculture (in the singular). Even when present in the mainstream, the heavy metal community will present itself in more or less subcultural ways, variably differentiating the "true" metalheads from the casual onlookers. Just as a subculture is not necessarily oppressed (Brown 2003), the concept should always be understood in an analytical sense, not as a concrete entity.

In the interviews, we found that whenever women metalheads described gendered experiences, they typically expressed that they had to specially prove themselves as "real" fans of the genre, by demonstrating knowledge of the genre, going to shows, and wearing suitable heavy metal clothing. This finding confirms the results of other studies that likewise found that women have a special need to prove themselves in the heavy metal community (Hutcherson and Haenfler 2010; Jocson-Singh 2019; Kelly 2019; Shadrack 2018), with additional intersectional issues for sexual (Wright 2015) and racial minorities (Dawes 2015a, 2020), among others. Demonstrating the value of gender theories based on the notion of doing gender as an expression of gender performativity and corroborating the findings from research on women as the Other in heavy metal (Allett 2010; Kitteringham 2014; Kummer 2016a, 2016b), women were therefore also said to rely, more than men would have to, on physical markers to (subjectively) feel and (objectively) act as well as to (intersubjectively) be perceived as metalheads. These conditions are found to be even more pronounced in historically conservative societies, where heavy metal as a whole is culturally suspect and remains very much an underground phenomenon (Torreiro 2020). As a result of its marginal positioning in a nonliberal context, heavy metal can then ironically become a stronger political force, offering resistance on a cultural level and duly rebelling against traditional practices involving gender inequity, sexism, and violence against women (Agung Daryana 2020; Kelly 2014; LeVine 2008; Varas-Díaz 2019).

Some differences were found, though not consistently, between the responses of the men and women interviewed in our study. To some extent, this lack of a clear differentiation along gender lines may be due to the fact that men today tend to agree with women and are well aware of the experiences women face in the world of heavy metal. Gender differences may also intersect with other dividing lines in the heavy metal subculture. Confirming the findings from scholars on the status of other minority metalheads besides women (Clifford-Napoleone 2015; Dawes 2012; Brown and Griffin 2014), we indeed found indications that the heavy metal community is multi-stratified, not only (though still predominantly) made up of white heterosexual men but also containing a measure of diversity in terms of gender, ethnicity, class, and sexual orientation, along with multiple forms of intersectionality (Dawes 2015a, 2015b) and cross-cultural variations (Córdoba and Cuchivague 2021;

Townsend 2020; Varas-Díaz et al. 2021). In line with the interview results that showed that other minorities in heavy metal besides women also feel a special need to prove themselves, our perspective of woman as the Other in de Beauvoir's (1952) terms could therefore be extended to a broader focus on underrepresented minorities in heavy metal as others.

We separately examined perceptions about flashing and moshing because they explicitly or, at least, implicitly concern gendered forms of conduct that potentially involve objectification. Asked if flashing can affect a woman's status in the metal community, there were mixed responses from men and women, though flashing was generally seen as less prevalent in contemporary heavy metal. By contrast, there was a strong consensus that women who participate in moshing at heavy metal shows deserve respect from the community precisely because it is seen as an aggressive physical activity. This finding confirms that moshing is a special way for women in heavy metal to become a part of a culture that is considered masculine (Riches 2012, 2014; Riches et al. 2013), experiencing participation as transformative (Lowles 2018) and thereby learning what it means to be a metalhead (Epp 2019). Among the interview respondents, not many women were found to engage in moshing (not many men did either), but given the acknowledged association of moshing with the characteristics of physicality and (masculine) aggression that are otherwise also typical of heavy metal music and its lifestyle, it can be argued that women metalheads mosh to find acceptance in an environment that they thereby explicitly acknowledge as (still) being dominated by men.

Conceptions and treatments of women as the Other, (self-)objectification, and defensive othering are variably expressed by the participants of our study. While moshing by women metalheads is favorably received, its acceptance is defined in masculine terms. Flashing is generally, but especially by women, viewed negatively and responded to by means of defensive othering, separating some women in heavy metal from other women. Such issues are all the more, not less, striking as more women today have been joining the heavy metal subculture, albeit with notable differences across its many subgenres (Hutcherson and Haenfler 2010; Rademacher 2015; Schaap and Berkers 2014; Townsend 2020; Weinstein 2016).

Changes over time are likewise relevant, for instance, in terms of the relative mainstreaming of thrash, death, and black metal, the increasing popularity of once more extreme metal genres, and the normalization of such genres as hair metal (which is today usually no longer even defined as heavy metal but considered part of rock), with all due implications in terms of gender and other issues (Elflein 2016; Howe et al. 2015; Kores 2020). It remains an open question, however, if these perceived differences and changes adequately reflect realized conditions, rather than idealizations, of the gender relations in heavy metal. With these qualifications in mind, the participants of our study agree that they think that the environment is generally becoming more accepting of women metalheads. A closer look at the relevance of our work with respect to the sociology of gender may clarify some of these puzzling issues.

Gender

In terms of the theoretical model that we relied on to frame our research, a number of issues emerge. The observed differences between men and women in the world of heavy metal broadly indicate the value of West and Zimmerman's (1987) notion of doing gender and the concept of othering based on de Beauvoir's (1952) idea of the Other and Judith Butler's (1990) related concept of gender performativity. Most clearly revealed in the research findings is the notion of women as the Other who recognize themselves as different from, and in some definite sense considered less than, the men in their culture. Women confronted with these gender dynamics will fight gender inequities by relying on men's ideas of belonging and participation to be accepted. This notion of portraying masculine qualities and characteristics in order to be taken seriously is displayed most clearly in the descriptions and experiences given by the women participants in our study, but is also indicated by the fact that the hypermasculinity of the heavy metal subculture is recognized across genders.

Revealing their mindset of woman as the Other in the heavy metal community, the women who participated in our research agreed that women who mosh gain more respect, even if they did not mosh themselves, in which sense women in metal who display masculine qualities are considered to be less othered than women who do not. Confirming the findings of other studies on moshing and gender (Riches 2012, 2014; Riches et al. 2013), women respondents more generally discussed how they felt they needed to prove themselves in many ways, including showing knowledge of the genre, going to shows, and wearing certain clothing. The relevance of dress and of knowing what heavy metal is all about, as necessary conditions for women to belong to the subculture, was ironically already underscored during the interviewing process, when the interviewer herself was questioned on how she dressed— professionally and, therefore precisely, inappropriately—during the first two face-to-face interviews, as well as subsequently when she would often be asked about her favorite metal bands and the metal shows she had attended.

Offering support for the value of the perspective of defensive othering, women in hypermasculine environments create their own sub-subculture, in which women who display masculine qualities are placed higher than women who do not and, in this sense, remain more feminine in their conduct. This idea was in our research especially revealed in the opinions expressed about moshing and flashing. Women who mosh, the study participants generally agree, receive more respect because they hold their own as "one of the guys." Conversely, flashing was broadly disapproved, especially by the women respondents. Women metalheads tended to be less condoning of women who engage in flashing as they see it as an at best unnecessary form of (sexual) self-objectification.

These results of our study indicate that a hierarchy of values exists in the heavy metal subculture, whereby men are placed above women, while women as a group are, in turn, hierarchically ordered among one another in such a way that women who mosh are located at the top, women who do not mosh or flash in the middle, and women who flash at the bottom of an imagined idealized order of heavy metal authenticity. The empirical data concerning moshing and flashing indicate the value of the theory of defensive othering as moshing women receive more respect and that at least some of the women respondents—and in any case women rather than men—distanced themselves from women who flash. At the same time, respondents recognize that the subculture is changing in a beneficial direction for women, thereby indicating their realization that heavy metal's conditions in terms of standards of gender equality were not good before and are still not as good as they can and should be.

The dynamics of gender in heavy metal inevitably exist in a broader culture of gender-related values. Thus, while not explicitly mentioned in the interviews, gender performativity in heavy metal remains important to consider inasmuch the gender expectations for men and women that exist outside of the subculture will—perhaps to an extent much greater than participants realize and would care to admit—also be brought into the heavy metal community. Women who are openly fans of a genre of music that is commonly associated with hypermasculinity and who proudly participate in a subculture dominated by men can impact how women metalheads are, as women, perceived in society at large. An appropriately holistic view of subcultures must take into account the wider context in which heavy metal exists.

Likewise, while the responses to the interviews did not include many (subjective) descriptions or experiences directly linked to objectification, there may (objectively) nonetheless be objectification present in the metal subculture. An implicit indication hereof was revealed in our study when some of the men in the interviews made impersonally formulated approving statements about flashing, arguing that some of "the guys" like it. These respondents may have expressed their own feelings but were prevented from providing a personalized positive assessment because they know it is not a very popular viewpoint, not to mention that the interviewer in this study is a woman.

The one clear instance when objectification was revealed in the interviews relates to the finding that some women in our study discussed having physical markers on their body (dress, hairstyle, tattoos) because they feel that they have to show that they too are metalheads. Invoking Judith Butler's (2004) idea of "bodily indicators," such markers indicate how women metalheads both have to engage in doing gender but also seek to undo it in a delicate balance of separation and belonging. This social pressure on women in heavy metal connects with the theory of self-objectification that holds that objectified members of society or a subgroup thereof may turn their own bodies into a project to reach a specific goal (in this case fitting into the heavy metal subculture) and thereby objectify their body and self. While this finding was not prevalent among many respondents, it was expressed exclusively by women.

Questions on gender are perceived differently in the various fan communities of heavy metal's many subgenres, including what is nowadays called extreme metal (such as death metal and black metal), traditional heavy metal (including 1980s thrash metal and 1970s hard rock), symphonic metal, hair metal, and folk metal, to name but a few. Not only are the musical stylings, lyrics, and images of these subgenres different, so are the behaviors and attitudes of their respective audiences as these subgenres tend to attract different fans in terms of gender, age, race/ethnicity, and other sociodemographic characteristics. Keeping such variations in mind, the general sentiment among the respondents is that women in heavy metal are today treated better and not sexualized as much as they once were, especially during the hedonistic and misogynist times of 1980s hair metal. As a result, the impression is clearly that women in heavy metal today are more equal and that they have been able to claim a place that is wholly their own. But the dynamics and conditions of gender in heavy metal may not be as clear-cut as its participants claim or hope them to be. We therefore need to reflect on the prospects of the development of a heavy metal feminism.

Feminism

As social science scholars, we are better equipped by training and expertise to study conditions and experiences but, typically, less concerned with reflecting on what it all means. Scholarship rooted in feminist thought, however, would fall short in terms of its ambitions if it would not also consider the normative implications of observed social realities. In this final section, we therefore wish to push further the analysis of where women in heavy metal find themselves today to contemplate if recent changes in heavy metal's gender dynamics point the way toward the development of a culture of feminism involving acceptance and integration.

Recent scholarship on women in heavy metal is divided over the question of whether or not a heavy metal feminism exists or, at least, is developing. Arguing in favor of the formation of feminism in heavy metal, the contemporary heavy metal scene is conceived by some scholars as providing a space of equality because it permits different performativities and understandings on gender that create real pathways toward inclusion (Riches 2015). Heavy metal, it is argued, can provide a site of empowerment where patriarchy can be destabilized and women liberated precisely because of the subculture's marginality (Savigny and Sleight 2015). So-called extreme forms of heavy metal, which are situated at society's outer margins because of their underground status, could therefore be especially powerful as sites where gender conventions can be overcome (Overell 2012, 2014). The internet may also have contributed to bring about more gender equality, or at least decrease gender inequality, in heavy metal. Under these circumstances, it has even been claimed that heavy metal is not "inherently" masculine (Hill 2016a, 2016b). Such a position not only overlooks the historically embedded (hyper)masculinity of heavy metal (Turbé 2016), but more broadly fails to understand that society and culture are, by definition, constructed realities that have no inherent properties but are nonetheless very real in their implications.

Other scholars, however, have rightly remained more cautious to argue that women metalheads continue to do gender on the variously masculine terms of men and need to continually balance between femininity and masculinity. The interview-based research by Nordström and Herz (2013) is especially useful and convincing in this respect by showing that women metalheads must critically engage in seeking to maintain femininity in a subculture that is highly masculine. Thus, women in heavy metal have to constantly "move their gender position to a greater extent than men" (p. 453). Similarly, the quantitative presence of women in heavy metal as musicians, though growing, has nonetheless been found to remain not only small but also primarily defined in masculine terms. Women singers in heavy metal, by example, will be either seen as adding a nonmetal, even a pop element to the music when they sing in a clean and high voice, or, conversely, perceived as acting like a man when they scream and growl (Ritlop 2020). Berkers and Schaap (2018) in this context speak of the "double-edged sword" of femininity on the part of women producing metal music because they can typically attain more visibility and attention only at the expense of not being taken as seriously as musicians.

Other research has likewise suggested that women musicians seeking to enter the world of heavy metal still face obstacles, both culturally in terms of style and disposition and structurally in terms of available social networks (Glitsos 2020; Miller 2014, 2016, 2017). These findings parallel other research areas that show that women can enter once more exclusive homosocial environments but only by behaving like men (Young et al. 2005). The question then is, both in terms of gender equality as well as sociologically, if women may lose anything of cultural or structural value in the process of acting like men.

More generally, while gender advances have surely been made in heavy metal, an ambivalence continues to exist on the implications of the increasingly gender-mixed climate of the subculture as a whole (Porrovecchio 2017; Savigny and Sleight 2015; Vasan 2011, 2016). Studies that are too naively positive (or negative) about gender conditions and other sociological aspects of heavy metal tend to be conducted by some of the music culture's participants who do not sufficiently step outside of their immediate music culture and therefore fail to see and comprehend critical ambiguities. Rather than recognizing relevant signs of ambivalence, such metal scholarship cannot but reflect the confusion it is meant to study. Fully absorbed in contradiction, it is then argued that even though "women are side-lined in this male-dominated and hypermasculine genre" (Hill 2016a, p. 1), heavy metal would nonetheless be "a culture that is relatively free from sexism" (Hill 2018, p. 265). Nothing could be further from the truth, of course, and any of the advances women have made in heavy metal need to be assessed alongside metal's continued sexism problems. That sexism in heavy metal, even today, is at times still very alive and all too well is demonstrated when a YouTube video of a panel talk on the very topic provoked a disturbing number of sexist comments, arguing that "real strong women don't whine on the internet about sexism", that heavy metal is not a "safe space" but "a place for moshing," and that "playing the victim makes you look weak and fragile" (BangerTV 2016).

Harmonizing with our research, Nordström and Herz (2013) have articulated the gender ambivalence in heavy metal in terms of the dichotomies women metalheads have to deal with to be especially knowledgeable about heavy metal. The authors show how women in the metal community constantly have to "navigate" between acting like a man and looking like a woman and finding oneself perceived to be insufficiently masculine for heavy metal and insufficiently feminine for the outside world (Nordström and Herz 2013). Based on the results of our research, it is indeed clear that the seeds of feminism in heavy metal are undoubtedly present and that the conditions for women in heavy metal today are more favorable than they once were in the days when the subculture was less diverse, demographically and otherwise.

The stated opinions of the interview respondents are rather straightforward in respect of noting the gender advances and feminist possibilities of heavy metal. However, as some of the respondents as participants of the heavy metal community also revealed how they have to navigate their gender in concrete circumstances, we must remain cautious about the actual realization of the aspired ideals of feminism in the metal subculture. We therefore suggest that a state of ambiguity exists in terms of women's place and role in the metal community. Although there are undeniable gains in the increasing involvement of women in heavy metal in recent years, judging from the thoughts expressed by metalheads themselves, there are both possibilities and obstacles toward the development of a veritable heavy metal feminism.

The increasing presence of women in heavy metal does not necessarily imply an integration of the genders, at least not inasmuch as heavy metal remains a homosocial space fostering social bonds among men, with women to some extent trying to fit in, but to another extent having to create their own subspaces. Invoking Georg Simmel's (1908) notion of the stranger, women in heavy metal thus remain simultaneously near and remote, accepted and othered, as they are always in, but not always of, the community. Noteworthy in this connection is that the demographic shifts that have taken place in today's rock and metal, with the music being able to attract fans from across different generations, are distinctly gendered. Heavy metal's cross-generational appeal in attracting parents and their children, by example, will typically involve fathers and sons, while bonding experiences between mothers and daughters at metal concerts, though not impossible (Bell 2021), until today are more rare.

The lack of clarity that exists among scholars concerning the role of gender in heavy metal, we argue, is the result of a failure to recognize the fundamental ambiguity that marks the role and place of women in the metal community. Indeed, judging from a number of topics that have been addressed in prior research, contributions framed as metal music studies or heavy metal scholarship too often do not move beyond the insider perspectives of its practitioners and are insufficiently divorced in their analysis from the participation and experiences of their respective authors as metalheads. Then the question of sexism in heavy metal is addressed such that the observation is made, with some apparent bewilderment, that "academic accounts and fan accounts are at odds on the answer" (Hill 2016a, p. 133), thereby failing to see that scholarship and insider perspectives do not even address the same question.

Adding to the confusion over gender and other aspects of heavy metal, there is a tendency in metal studies to develop and counteract arguments on the basis of how much one knows about heavy metal (especially the music), rather than relying on considerations of why certain findings are relevant within a particular framework of inquiry. Absent a clear scholarly perspective that not only leads to ask the right questions and find the best answers but also clarifies how one can make sense of findings, metal scholars then accept only that which harmonizes with their self-understanding of heavy metal, while those findings that clash therewith are seen as merely "imagined" (Hill 2016a). More generally, drawing on an expertise that is rooted in one's knowledge as a metalhead will come at a great cost for the development of scholarship when it directs the manner in which a research question can be answered, rather than being guided by theory and methodology.

Problems plaguing the development of academic work on heavy metal could be avoided if scholars would conduct their research in the context of the existing disciplines of the social and behavioral sciences and/or develop their work from within the broader and more established fields of study on popular culture, gender, and other relevant thematic areas. Then studies of heavy metal can be strengthened by developing useful disciplinary grounding in theory and methodology (in terms of approach) and establishing fruitful connections with the wider themes to which they are related (as subject matter). Such positioning would also prevent studies on heavy metal from being isolated from other relevant scholarship, avoiding the danger of being seen as merely a way to give heavy metal an air of respectability, which no metalhead may even have asked for.

Community and Society

Based on our research, women in heavy metal still have to do gender, at times even precisely when they seek to undo it. One can safely assume that women metalheads (like men) enjoy heavy metal because they like the music irrespective of its masculine qualities. But it is one thing to like a style of music, quite another to reveal this appreciation openly and to actively participate in a community that is real rather than merely imagined. What women metalheads in this sense display even more clearly than the men is a sense of defiance and rebelliousness as joining the subculture itself also defies conventional gender expectations. Yet, inasmuch as notions of masculinity still persist in heavy metal, women metalheads will continue to feel a special need for belonging and recognition despite their increasing strength in numbers. It is telling to observe in this respect that some of the women interviewed for our research may have sought to prove themselves by providing lengthy and informative answers, while some of the men at times appeared rather disinterested even as they were in a position to discuss aspects of their favorite style of music.

Taking a look at gender issues in the heavy metal community beyond our immediate research findings, the ambiguities revealed in the interviews are also reflected in discussions on women metalheads in the popular media. In the music press, the changing status of women in metal is indeed addressed quite often, usually in terms of an increase in the number of women as performers, especially singers, and, to a lesser extent, as fans of the genre (Brown 2016; Kelly 2011, 2019). While such media reports often comment favorably on the increasing involvement of women in metal, they also typically point out continued difficulties, especially the purported sexism of the heavy metal community. Ironically, however, the manner in which these media reports are phrased is indicative of the fact that women in metal are still considered unusual (Loye 2015). Affirming a process of othering by means of gender marking, most notably, these accounts differentiate specifically designated women performers and women fans in heavy metal from a community that is described in nongendered terms, though known to be made up mostly of men.

Revealing broader societal conditions concerning gender, sexism, and popular culture, media accounts typically discuss so-called "female-fronted" metal bands and "all-girl" or "all-female" groups (Lapolla 2016), designations that have been criticized as suggesting an unjustifiably co-herent and distinctly sexist category that is set apart from all other heavy metal (Chapstick 2018; Cownley 2020). Thus, similar to how women's sports is differentiated from sports, so there is a gendered separation of female-fronted heavy metal (specifically) from heavy metal (in general). When women are involved in a traditionally masculine environment, in other words, their activities are gendered and in special need of having to demonstrate their value. Consequently, when the presence of women as fans and performers of heavy metal is discussed in the media, it typically occurs in unexpected contexts, such as the women's metal music scene in Botswana (Shiakallis 2015), the tribulations of an all-women Indonesian metal group (Leigh 2019), a Buddhist nun joining a Taiwanese heavy metal band (Jennings 2021), and the so-called girls metal band boom in Japanese heavy metal (Baku 2018). Such media portrayals have in common that they reaffirm a curiosity aspect of women as metalheads and metal musicians (Cooper 2020; Kelly 2011).

Based on information provided in popular news media, the ambiguities of gender advancement in heavy metal are also revealed in interviews with women musicians from the metal community, who receive recognition but also face continued obstacles (Goodman 2020). For instance, Angela Gossow, the now legendary former singer of extreme metal band Arch Enemy, has stated that it is today "easier for women to actually get into bands, because it's been proven that it works," but she also added that "in terms of being seen as a sex object first, it hasn't changed, it's still the same old game. People com-ment on your looks first before they listen to what you do" (in Evans 2010). Similarly, when frontwoman Maria Brink of American metal band In This Moment was asked if she had to prove herself being a woman in metal, she responded, "I don't think so," but she then also went on to say, "I've had 500 people scream, "Show me your tits!" at Ozzfest at the same time. I used to let that have power over me and I used to think that I had to be really tough and scream at the crowd and be like a boy, to be taken seriously. It was all bullshit!" (Blabbermouth 2014).

Likewise indicating continued objectification is the fact that the media often rate women performers in heavy metal, sometimes in highly sexualized ways, in comparison with one another, but not in relation to men performers. The magazine *Revolver*, by example, regularly publishes a list of the "25 Hottest Chicks" in hard rock and metal. Such instances affirm that sexual objectification in heavy metal remains a concern (Kelly 2011), even though the musicianship of women in heavy metal bands is nowadays also recognized (Cooper 2020). Likewise, it can be observed that the growing presence of women as heavy metal musicians, which at least questions the notion that the sounds and style of heavy metal music might inherently be masculine (Friesen and Epstein 1994), has not always brought about a parallel increase in women as metal fans.

The holistic perspective we suggested in terms of the embeddedness of subcultures in a broader social context also leads us to place the continued advances women metalheads make within the evolving culture of masculinity that exists among the men of metal. As both participants and scholars of heavy metal have suggested, important changes have taken place in the masculinity that is at work in the subculture and its various subgenres (Scott 2016; Weinstein 2016). As already during the formative years of heavy metal the subculture's masculinity may not have been entirely uniform (Jones 2018; Lind 2013), different forms and degrees of masculinity exist today, some of them allowing more readily for women to express themselves on their own terms than others. However, even in some genres of contemporary heavy metal where the inclusion of women performers has become standard (e.g., symphonic metal bands featuring women singers), women are not always included and recognized as a fellow member, but are sometimes perceived as the Other, at other times as more similar, and most typically as having to navigate gender roles. In our research, these variations and their uncertain implications were reflected in some of the interviewed men being more aware of women's status in heavy metal than others, which in itself is an indication of the ambiguities of heavy metal feminism.

Besides changing conceptions of masculinity, finally, also to be considered are the prevailing cultural notions on gender as more or less binary or fluid. Until today, the world of heavy metal remains largely binarily structured as consisting of men and, to a lesser but growing extent, women. However, some transgender manifestations should be noted as well. All-women tribute bands, such as Lez Zeppelin, AC/DShe, and The Iron Maidens, can be argued to disrupt masculinity precisely by enacting masculine roles (Gregory 2013). Other gender-fluid manifestations in heavy metal also exist, such as the transgressive androgyny of performers and fans of some of metal's contemporary subgenres (de Gallier 2016), the opportunities the metal scene can provide as a space for queer people (Clifford-Napoleone 2015; Solomon 2021), and the broadening of lyrical themes far beyond the boundaries of conventional masculine themes, ranging from the macho masculinity of traditional British metal (Weinstein 2009) and the screaming agonies of broken masculinity and angst in nu metal (Rafalovich 2006) to the romantic masculinity of goth metal (Weinstein 2016).

Additionally complicating the gender picture of contemporary heavy metal, mention can be made of the gendered use of horror themes in some forms of heavy metal (Digioia 2020) and, perhaps most clearly though not as common, the coming-out of transgender heavy metal fans (Fisher 2016) and musicians (Fort 2017; Grow 2017). Although most heavy metal is surely not akin to alternative rock in its political ambitions or to glam and goth rock in terms of their embrace of notions of gender fluidity, at least a few cracks can be observed in contemporary metal's binary gender code.

In sum, studying gender in the heavy metal community touches on many an aspect concerning the evolving status of women and the ongoing tension between sexism and feminism that have been duly recognized in sociology and gender studies. The objectives of our study and other pertinent literature on the gender dynamics in popular culture should therefore readily resonate with scholars studying similar issues in other areas of social life. Because of their relevance, the dynamics of gender also need to be studied as a serious matter among scholars in sociology and other disciplines examining the world of popular culture. The study of gender in popular music cultures, such as heavy metal, should find its rightful place in, and contribute to show the value of, this literature, as our book hopes to have demonstrated.

The very fact that many of the patterns and dynamics of what we and others have found in the heavy metal subculture has also been found elsewhere in society shows the undeniable value of pop culture to sociology and related fields. As there still is a need to take heavy metal, music (sub)cultures, and popular culture more seriously from a scholarly viewpoint, our study provided relevant data about the experiences for women whose identity and self are deeply engrained in a homosocial environment. These issues are not only useful from the viewpoint of the study of music and culture and the human need for play but also touch on the potentially harmful consequences of the continued difficulties and objectification of women in heavy metal and the sexist implications thereof. Issues of gender and gender inequity are worth exploring not only in heavy metal but also across different genres of music and other areas of popular culture as well. As gender respect and equality cannot be legislated from above, the dynamics of gender in the wide world of pop culture will not be without broader relevance, of interest to scholars from a wide range of fields and perspectives. Music and other forms of popular culture provide a rich area of study to examine the degree and direction of gender advances while also observing to what extent and how the song remains the same.

APPENDIX: INTERVIEW GUIDE

- Age:
- Race:
- Sex/gender:
- How long have you been a metal fan?
- What made you become a fan of this particular genre?
- What are some of your favorite bands?
- How many (metal) concerts have you been to?
- What does it mean to you to be a real metal fan?
- What are, according to you, the main characteristics of a metal fan?
- How does a fan become accepted into the group in your opinion?
- How would you describe the metal fan base as a group overall?
- How would you describe interactions between metal fans at shows?
- How would you describe the interactions in a mosh pit?
- Would you consider the heavy metal fan culture as a whole to be dominated by men or overly masculine?
- Do you think your gender (as a man/woman) has affected your acceptance into the group? How?
- When a woman flashes at a concert, how do you think that affects her status?
- When a woman moshes at a concert, how do you think that affects her status?
- Do you think it is generally harder (or not) for a woman to be accepted as a metal fan than for a man?
- Is there any other information you would like to share with me?

BIBLIOGRAPHY

3 Inches of Blood. 2012. *Long Live Heavy Metal* (musical recording). Century Media Records.

Agung Daryana, Hinhin, Aquarini Priyatna, and Raden Muhamad Mulyadi. 2020. "The New Metal Men: Exploring Model of Alternative Masculinity in the Bandung Metal Scene." *Masculinities and Social Change* 9(2): 148–73.

Allett, Nicola F. 2010. " 'Love's Labours': Extreme Metal Music and Its Feeling Community." PhD thesis, University of Warwick. https://wrap.warwick.ac.uk/3110/1/WRAP_THESIS_Allett_2010.pdf.

Anderson, Eric. 2008. " 'I Used to Think Women Were Weak': Orthodox Masculinity, Gender Segregation, and Sport." *Sociological Forum* 23(2): 257–80.

Armstrong, Elizabeth A., Laura Hamilton, and Brian Sweeney. 2006. "Sexual Assault on Campus: A Multilevel, Integrative Approach to Party Rape." *Social Problems* 53(4): 483–99.

Arnett, Jeffrey J. 1996. *Metalheads: Heavy Metal Music and Adolescent Alienation*. Boulder, CO: Westview Press.

Åström, Berit. 2015. "The Symbolic Annihilation of Mothers in Popular Culture: Single Father and the Death of the Mother." *Feminist Media Studies* 15(4): 593–607.

Babbie, Earl. 2010. "Qualitative Data Analysis." Pp. 393–420 in his *The Practice of Social Research*, 12th ed. Belmont, CA: Wadsworth.

Baker, Charley, and Brian Brow. 2016. "Suicide, Self-Harm and Survival Strategies in Contemporary Heavy Metal Music: A Cultural and Literary Analysis." *Journal of Medical Humanities* 37(1): 1–17.

Baku. 2018. "We Will Rock You: Japanese Heavy Metal Girl Bands." *Baku Magazine*, July 30, 2018. https://baku-magazine.com/everything-else/top-five-japanese-heavy-metal-girl-bands/.

BangerTV. 2016. "Sexism in Metal Panel Discussion." YouTube, streamed live on September 28, 2016 (archived). https://www.youtube.com/watch?v=S5jaItN3DoM.

Barron, Lee. 2013. "Dworkin's Nightmare: Pornogrind as the Sound of Feminist Fears." Pp. 66–82 in *Heavy Metal: Controversies and Countercultures*, edited by Titus Hjelm, Keith Kahn-Harris, and Mark LeVine. Sheffield, UK: Equinox.

Becknell, Milton E., Michael W. Firmin, Chi-En Hwang, David M. Fleetwood, Kristie L. Tate, and Gregory D. Schwab. 2008. "Effects of Listening to Heavy Metal Music on College Women: A Pilot Study." *College Student Journal* 42(1): 24–35.

Bell, Susannah. 2021. "At a Heavy Metal Concert, Balancing Independence with Boundaries." *New York Times*, February 5, 2021. https://www.nytimes.com/2021/02/05/well/family/at-a-heavy-metal-concert-balancing-independence-with-boundaries.html.

Berg, Bruce L., and Kimberly J. Budnick. 1986. "Defeminization of Women in Law Enforcement: A New Twist in the Traditional Police Personality." *Journal of Police Science & Administration* 14: 314–19.

Berkers, Pauwke, and Julian Schaap. 2018. *Gender Inequality in Metal Music Production*. Bingley, UK: Emerald.

Bernard, H. Russell, 2013. *Social Research Methods: Qualitative and Quantitative Approaches*, 2nd ed. Thousand Oaks, CA: Sage.

Bird, Sharon R. 1996. "Welcome to the Men's Club: Homosociality and the Maintenance of Hegemonic Masculinity." *Gender and Society* 10(2): 120–32.

Blabbermouth. 2014. "In This Moment's Maria Brink: 'When I Walk Out on Stage Now, I'm Confident." Blabbermouth, December 2, 2014. http://www.blabbermouth.net/news/in-this-moments-maria-brink-when-i-walk-out-on-stage-now-im-confident/.

Blott, Jonathan. 2021. "High Spirits: Heavy Metal and Mental Health." *Lancet Psychiatry* 8(2): 105–7.

Bolay, Jordan. 2019. "'Their Song Was Partial; But the Harmony [...] Suspended Hell': Intertextuality, Voice and Gender in Milton/Symphony X's *Paradise Lost*." *Metal Music Studies* 5(1): 5–20.

Bradburn, Norman, Seymour Sudman, and Brian Wansink. 2004. *Asking Questions: The Definitive Guide to Questionnaire Design—For Market Research, Political Polls, and Social and Health Questionnaires*. San Francisco, CA: Jossey-Bass.

Brady, Anita, and Tony Schirato. 2011. *Understanding Judith Butler*. Thousand Oaks, CA: Sage.

Brown, Andy R. 2003. "Heavy Metal and Subcultural Theory: A Paradigmatic Case of Neglect?" Pp. 209–22 in *The Post-Subcultures Reader*, edited by David Muggleton and Rupert Weinzierl. Oxford, UK: Berg.

———. 2011. "Heavy Genealogy: Mapping the Currents, Contraflows and Conflicts of the Emergent Field of Metal Studies, 1978–2010." *Journal for Cultural Research* 15(3): 213–42.

———. 2016. "'Girls Like Metal, Too!': Female Reader's Engagement with the Masculinist Culture of the Tabloid Metal Magazine." Pp. 163–81 in *Heavy Metal, Gender and Sexuality: Interdisciplinary Approaches*, edited by Florian Heesch and Niall Scott. Abingdon, UK: Routledge.

Brown, Andy R., and Christine Griffin. 2014. "'A Cockroach Preserved in Amber': The Significance of Class in Critics Representations of Heavy Metal Music and its Fans." *Sociological Review* 62(4): 719–41.

Bryson, Bethany. 1996. "Anything but Heavy Metal: Symbolic Exclusion and Musical Dislikes." *American Sociological Review* 61(5): 884–99.

Butler, Judith. 1990. *Gender Trouble*. New York: Routledge.

———. 1993. *Bodies That Matter: On the Discursive Limits of "Sex."* New York: Routledge.

———. 2004. *Undoing Gender*. New York: Routledge.

Calleja, Jen, Willars Liv, and Heather Perkins. 2015. "Op-Ed: Why There Are So Few Women on Festival Bills and Why That Needs to Change—Now." Pitchfork, June 26, 2015. https://pitchfork.com/thepitch/816-op-ed-why-there-are-so-few-women-on-festival-bills-and-why-that-needs-to-change-now/.

Caporale, Micco. 2018. "This Heavy Metal Singer Became a Lawyer Fighting Sexism in Music." Vice, April 9, 2018. https://www.vice.com/en/article/43bnqg/this-heavy-metal-singer-became-a-lawyer-fighting-sexism-in-music.

Chaker, Sarah, and Florian Heesch. 2016. "Female Metal Singers: A Panel Discussion with Sabina Classen, Britta Görtz, Angela Gossow." Pp. 133–44 in *Heavy Metal, Gender and Sexuality: Interdisciplinary Approaches*, edited by Florian Heesch and Niall Scott. Abingdon, UK: Routledge.

Chapstick, Kelsey. 2018. "Why It's Important to Stop Using 'Female-Fronted' as a Metal Genre Right Now." MetalSucks, February 7. http://www.metalsucks.net/2018/02/07/why-its-important-to-stop-using-female-fronted-as-a-metal-genre-right-now/.

Christe, Ian. 2003. *Sound of the Beast: The Complete Headbanging History of Heavy Metal.* New York: Harper Entertainment.

Clifford-Napoleone, Amber. 2015. *Queerness in Heavy Metal Music: Metal Bent.* Abingdon, UK: Routledge.

Cohen, Sara. 1997. "Men Making a Scene: Rock Music and the Production of Gender." Pp. 17–36 in *Sexing the Groove: Popular Music and Gender*, edited by Sheila Whitely. New York: Routledge.

———. 2001. "Popular Music, Gender and Sexuality." Pp. 226–42 in *The Cambridge Companion to Pop and Rock*, edited by Simon Frith, Will Straw, and John Street. Cambridge: Cambridge University Press.

Cooper, Ali. 2020. "20 Women in Metal Who Don't Need a Microphone to Take Center Stage: Power to the Ladies Who Don't Wield a Mic." Alternative Press, September 14. https://www.altpress.com/features/best-women-in-metal/.

Córdoba, Jesús Antonio, and Karen Ortiz Cuchivague. 2021. "Female Participation in Colombian Metal: An Initial Approach." *Metal Music Studies* 7(1): 159–70.

Cownley, Emma. 2020. "Will 'Female-Fronted Metal' Finally Die in 2020?," *Metal Hammer,* January 3. https://www.loudersound.com/features/will-female-fronted-metal-finally-die-in-2020.

Craig, Jane M., and Rick R. Jacobs. 1985. "The Effect of Working with Women on Male Attitudes toward Female Firefighters." *Basic and Applied Social Psychology* 6(1): 61–74.

Curry, Colleen. 2017. "Heavy Metal Singer Stops Concert to Defend Woman from Sexual Assault." Global Citizen, August 21. https://www.globalcitizen.org/en/content/heavy-metal-singer-stops-concert-to-defend-fan-fro/.

Davis, Mark H., Sal Capobianco, and Linda A. Kraus. 2010. "Gender Differences in Responding to Conflict in the Workplace: Evidence from a Large Sample of Working Adults." *Sex Roles* 63: 500–514.

Dawes, Laina. 2012. *What Are You Doing Here? A Black Woman's Life and Liberation in Heavy Metal.* Brooklyn, NY: Bazillion Points.

———. 2015a. "Challenging an 'Imagined Community': Discussions (Or Lack Thereof) of Black and Queer Experiences Within Heavy Metal Culture." *Metal Music Studies* 1(3): 385–93.

———. 2015b. "Heavy Metal Feminism." Hazlitt, August 17. https://hazlitt.net/blog/heavy-metal-feminism.

———. 2020. "Fighting Against Racism in Metal Is More Important Than Ever." *Metal Hammer,* June 9. https://www.loudersound.com/features/fighting-against-racism-in-metal-is-more-important-than-ever.

de Beauvoir, Simone. 1952. *The Second Sex*, edited and translated by H. M. Parshley. New York: Alfred A. Knopf.

Deflem, Mathieu. 2015. "Lady Gaga—The Scream of a Rock Star." Pp. 73–93 in *Pop-Frauen der Gegenwart: Körper–Stimme–Image*, edited by Christa Brüstle. Bielefeld, Germany: Transcript.

————. 2017. *Lady Gaga and the Sociology of Fame: The Rise of a Pop Star in an Age of Celebrity.* New York: Palgrave Macmillan.

————. 2020. "Popular Culture and Social Control: The Moral Panic on Music Labeling." *American Journal of Criminal Justice* 45(1): 2–24.

de Gallier, Thea. 2016. "Dude Looks Like a Lady: The Power of Androgyny in Metal." *Metal Hammer*, February 12. https://www.loudersound.com/features/dude-looks-like-a-lady-the-power-of-androgyny-in-metal.

Denski, Stan, and David Sholle. 1992. "Metal Men and Glamour Boys: Gender Performance in Heavy Metal." Pp. 41–60 in *Men and Masculinity in the Media*, edited by Steve Craig. Newbury Park, CA: Sage.

DeVault, Marjorie L. 2002. "Talking and Listening from Women's Standpoint: Feminist Strategies for Interviewing and Analysis." Pp. 88–111 in *Qualitative Research Methods*, edited by Darien Weinberg. Malden, MA: Blackwell.

DiGioia, Amanda. 2016a. "Lechery, Lycanthropy, and Little Red Riding Hood in Type O Negative's 'Wolf Moon' (Including Zoanthropic Paranoia)." *Metal Music Studies* 2(2): 233–43.

————. 2016b. "A Cry in the Dark: The Howls of Wolves in Horror and Heavy Metal Music." *Horror Studies* 7(2): 293–306.

————. 2020. "Nameless, but Not Blameless: Motherhood in Finnish Heavy Metal Music." *Metal Music Studies* 6(2): 237–55.

DiGioia, Amanda, and Lyndsay Helfrich. 2018. "'I'm Sorry, but It's True, You're Bringin' on the Heartache': The Antiquated Methodology of Deena Weinstein." *Metal Music Studies* 4(2): 365–74.

Doerer, Kristen. 2018. "The NFL's Problem with Violence Against Women: A Story of Profit and Apathy." *Guardian*, December 7. https://www.theguardian.com/sport/2018/dec/07/the-nfls-problem-with-violence-against-women-a-story-of-profit-and-apathy.

Doucette, Whitney. 2018. *Hypermasculinity in the Heavy Metal Subculture.* Capstone Projects and Master's Theses. Monterey Bay: California State University. https://digitalcommons.csumb.edu/caps_thes_all/426.

Elflein, Dietmar. 2016. "Never Say Die! Ozzy Osbourne as a Male Role Model." Pp. 71–83 in *Heavy Metal, Gender, and Sexuality: Interdisciplinary Approaches*, edited by F. Heesch and N. Scott. Abingdon, UK: Routledge.

Engels, Friedrich. 1884. *The Origin of the Family, Private Property and the State.* Online English translation edition in the Marx & Engels Internet Archive. https://www.marxists.org/archive/marx/works/1884/origin-family/.

Epp, André. 2017. "Diversity in Metal Politics." Pp. 81–98 in *Connecting Metal to Culture: Unity in Disparity*, edited by Mika Elovaara and Bryan Bardine. Bristol, UK: Intellect.

————. 2019. "The Mosh Pit—an Area for Excess or a Place of Learning?," *Metal Music Studies* 5(1): 107–14.

Evans, Kristy. 2010. "Arch Enemy's Angela Gossow: 'I'm the Boss.'" Global Comment, March 10. http://globalcomment.com/arch-enemys-angela-gossow-im-the-boss/.

Ezzell, Matthew B. 2009. "'Barbie Dolls' on the Pitch: Identity Work, Defensive Othering, and Inequality in Women's Rugby." *Social Problems* 56(1): 111–31.

Fine, Gary Alan, and Sherryl Kleinman. 1979. "Rethinking Subculture: An Interactionist Analysis." *American Journal of Sociology* 85(1): 1–20.

Fisher, Jessica. 2016. "On Being Transgender in the Metal Community." Metal Insider blog post, July 12. https://www.metalinsider.net/guest-blog/on-being-transgender-in-the-metal-community.

Flansburg, Glenn. 2021. *Performing Gender: Hell Hath No Fury Like a Woman Horned*. MA thesis, University of Oklahoma. https://shareok.org/handle/11244/327529.

Fleetwood, Jennifer. 2014. "Keeping Out of Trouble: Female Crack Cocaine Dealers in England." *European Journal of Criminology* 11(1): 91–109.

Forrest, Rebecca. 2010. "Mud Shark: Groupies and the Construction of the Heavy Metal Rock God." Pp. 135–48 in *The Metal Void: First Gatherings*, edited by Niall W. R. Scott and Imke Von Helden. Oxford: Inter-Disciplinary Press.

Fort, Patrick. 2017. "Election of Transgender Lawmaker in Virginia Makes History." NPR, November 7. https://www.npr.org/2017/11/07/562679573/election-of-transgender-lawmaker-in-virginia-makes-history.

Friesen, Bruce K. 1990. "Powerlessness in Adolescence: Exploiting Heavy Metal Listeners." Pp. 65–77 in *Marginal Conventions: Popular Culture, Mass Media and Social Deviance*, edited by C. R. Saunders. Bowling Green, OH: Bowling Green University Press.

Friesen, Bruce K., and Jonathon S. Epstein. 1994. "Rock 'n' Roll Ain't Noise Pollution: Artistic Conventions and Tensions in the Major Subgenres of Heavy Metal Music." *Popular Music and Society* 18(3): 1–17.

Friesen, Bruce K., and Warren Helfrich. 1998. "Social Justice and Sexism for Adolescents: A Content Analysis of Lyrical Themes and Gender Presentations in Canadian Heavy Metal Music, 1985–1991." Pp. 263–85 in *Youth Culture: Identity in a Postmodern World*, edited by J. Epstein. Malden, MA: Blackwell.

Gaines, Donna. 1998. *Teenage Wasteland: Suburbia's Dead End Kids*. Chicago: University of Chicago Press.

Gardenour Walter, Brenda, Gabby Riches, Dave Snell, and Bryan Bardine (eds.). 2016. *Heavy Metal Studies and Popular Culture*. Basingstoke, UK: Palgrave Macmillan.

Genz, Stéphanie. 2012. "Teaching Gender and Popular Culture." Pp. 122–37 in *Teaching Gender*, edited by Alice Ferrebe and Fiona Tolan. London: Palgrave Macmillan.

Glesne, Corrine. 2011. *Becoming Qualitative Researchers: An Introduction*. 4th edition. Boston, MA: Pearson Education.

Glitsos, Laura. 2020. "'Sticky Business': An Examination of Female Musicians in the Context of Perth's Metal Community." *Popular Music & Society* 43(1): 93–113.

Goffman, Erving. 1979. *Gender Advertisements*. Cambridge, MA: Harvard University Press.

Goodman, Eleanor. 2020. "Does Metal Have a Sexism Problem?" *Metal Hammer*, March 6. https://www.loudersound.com/features/does-metal-have-a-sexism-problem.

Goossens, Didier. 2019. *"Māori Metal": Analysing Decolonial Glocalisation in the Themes, Performances and Discourses Surrounding Alien Weaponry's Debut Album Tū (2018)*. Master's thesis, KU Leuven. https://www.scriptiebank.be/scriptie/2019/maori-metal-analysing-decolonial-glocalisation-themes-performances-and-discourses.

Gracyk, Theodore. 2016. "Heavy Metal: Genre? Style? Subculture?" *Philosophy Compass* 11(12): 775–85.

Granholm, Kennet. 2019. "Why All That Satanist Stuff in Heavy Metal?," Pp. 122–26 in *Hermes Explains: Thirty Questions about Western Esotericism*, edited by Marco Pasi, Peter Forshaw, and Wouter Hanegraaff. Amsterdam: Amsterdam University Press.

Grant, Judith. 1996. "Bring the Noise: Hypermasculinity in Heavy Metal and Rap." *Journal of Social Philosophy* 27(2): 5–31.

Gregory, Georgina. 2013. "Transgender Tribute Bands and the Subversion of Male Rites of Passage through the Performance of Heavy Metal Music." *Journal for Cultural Research* 17(1): 21–36.

Griffin, Hollis. 2014. "Hair Metal Redux: Gendering Nostalgia and Revising History on VH1." *Journal of Popular Film & Television* 42(2): 71–80.

Grow, Kory. 2017. "Life of Agony's Mina Caputo: From Metal Alpha Male to Trans Role Model." *Rolling Stone*, April 27. https://www.rollingstone.com/music/music-features/life-of-agonys-mina-caputo-from-metal-alpha-male-to-trans-role-model-198913/.

Gruzelier, Jonathan. 2007. "Moshpit Menace and Masculine Mayhem." Pp. 59–75 in *Oh Boy! Masculinities and Popular Music*, edited by Freya Jarman-Ivens. New York: Routledge.

Guajardo, Salomon A. 2016. "Women in Policing: A Longitudinal Assessment of Female Officers in Supervisory Positions in the New York City Police Department." *Women & Criminal Justice* 26(1): 20–36.

Guberman, Daniel. 2020. "Patriarchy, Cross-Dressing, Agency and Violence: Women and the Pedagogical Opportunities in Heavy Metal." Pp. 178–93 in *Popular Music in the Classroom: Essays for Instructors*, edited by David Whitt. Jefferson, NC: McFarland.

Habermas, Jürgen. (1970) 1988. *On the Logic of the Social Sciences*. Cambridge, MA: MIT Press.

Haenfler, Ross. 2010. "Heavy Metal: Moral Panics, Satanic Scares, and Moral Entrepreneurs." Pp. 57–70 in his *Goths, Gamers, & Grrrls: Deviance and Youth Subcultures*. New York: Oxford University Press.

Hällsten, Martin, Christofer Edling, and Jens Rydgren. 2019. "School's Out Forever? Heavy Metal Preferences and Higher Education. *PLoS One* 14(3): e0213716.

Halnon, Karen B. 2006. "Heavy Metal Carnival and Dis-alienation: The Politics of Grotesque Realism." *Symbolic Interaction* 29(1): 33–48.

Hauser, Orlee. 2011. "'We Rule the Base Because We're Few': 'Lone Girls' in Israel's Military." *Journal of Contemporary Ethnography* 40(6): 623–51.

Heesch, Florian, and Niall Scott (eds.). 2016. *Heavy Metal, Gender and Sexuality: Interdisciplinary Approaches*. Abingdon, UK: Routledge.

Helfrich, Lyndsay. 2017. *"I Wanna Rock": A Critique of Gender Essentialism in Metal Music Scholarship*. MA thesis, University of Saskatchewan. https://core.ac.uk/download/pdf/226117674.pdf.

Henningsen, David D., Mary L. Miller, and Kathleen S. Valde. 2006. "Gender Differences in Perceptions of Women's Sexual Interest during Cross-Sex Interactions: An Application of Cognitive Valence Theory." *Sex Roles* 54: 821–29.

Heritage, Gareth. 2016. "Accept(ing) the Other (Metallic[a]) Hypermasculine Image: Case Studies towards an Alternative Understanding of Hypermasculinity in the Aesthetics of 1980s Heavy Metal." *Metal Music Studies* 2(1): 57–68.

Hickam, Brian, and Jeremy Wallach. 2011. "Female Authority and Dominion: Discourse and Distinctions of Heavy Metal Scholarship." *Journal for Cultural Research* 15(3): 255–77.

Hill, Rosemary L. 2016a. *Gender, Metal and the Media: Women Fans and the Gendered Experience of Music*. Basingstoke, UK: Palgrave Macmillan.

———. 2016b. "Masculine Pleasure? Women's Encounters with Hard Rock and Metal Music." Pp. 277–93 in *Global Metal Music and Culture Studies: Current Directions in Metal Studies*, edited by Andy R. Brown, Karl Spracklen, Keith Kahn-Harris and Niall W. R. Scott. New York: Routledge.

———. 2016c. "'Power Has a Penis': Cost Reduction, Social Exchange and Sexism in Metal—Reviewing the Work of Sonia Vasan." *Metal Music Studies* 2(3): 263–71.

———. 2018. "Metal and Sexism." *Metal Music Studies* 4(2): 265–79.

Hoad, Catherine. 2016. "We Are the Sons of the Southern Cross: Gendered Nationalisms and Imagined Community in Australian Extreme Metal." *Journal of World Popular Music* 3(1): 90–107.

Hooton, Christopher. 2014. "Staind Frontman Aaron Lewis Stops Mid-Song to Call Crowd Out for 'Molesting' Crowd-Surfing Teen Girl." *Independent*, June 3. https://www.independent.co.uk/arts-entertainment/music/news/staind-frontman-stops-mid-song-to-call-crowd-out-for-molesting-crowd-surfing-girl-9479501.html.

Horton, Aaron D. 2021. "Gender and Non-Conformity in German and Japanese Metal Music and Subculture." Chapter 12 in *German-East Asian Encounters and Entanglements: Affinity in Culture and Politics Since 1945*, edited by Joanne Miyang Cho. New York: Routledge.

Howe, Tasha R., and Howard S. Friedman. 2014. "Sex and Gender in the 1980s Heavy Metal Scene: Groupies, Musicians, and Fans Recall Their Experiences." *Sexuality & Culture* 18(3): 608–29.

Howe, Tasha R., Christopher L. Aberson, Howard S. Friedman, Sarah E. Murphy, Esperanza Alcazar, Edwin J. Vazquez, and Rebekah Becker. 2015. "Three Decades Later: The Life Experiences and Mid-Life Functioning of 1980s Heavy Metal Groupies, Musicians, and Fans." *Self and Identity* 14(5): 602–26.

Huffman, Matt L. 2013. "Organizations, Managers, and Wage Inequality." *Sex Roles* 68: 216–22.

Hutcherson, Ben, and Ross Haenfler. 2010. "Musical Genre as a Gendered Process: Authenticity in Extreme Metal." *Studies in Symbolic Interaction* 35(5): 101–21.

International Society for Metal Music Studies. n.d. Accessed February 8, 2021. https://www.metalstudies.org/.

Jennings, Ralph. 2021. "This Is What Happens when a Buddhist Nun Joins a Heavy Metal Band." *Los Angeles Times*, January 29. https://www.latimes.com/world-nation/story/2021-01-29/when-a-buddhist-nun-joins-a-heavy-metal-band-spirits-rise.

Jocson-Singh, Joan M. 2016. *Individual Thought Patterns: Women in New York's Extreme Metal Music Scene*. MA thesis, Hunter College. https://academicworks.cuny.edu/hc_sas_etds/134/.

———. 2019. "Vigilante Feminism as a Form of Musical Protest in Extreme Metal Music." *Metal Music Studies* 5(2): 263–73.

Jones, Simon. 2018. "*Kerrang!* Magazine and the Representation of Heavy Metal Masculinities (1981–95)." *Metal Music Studies* 4(3): 459–80.

Kelly, Kim. 2011. "The Never-Ending Debate over Women in Metal and Hard Rock." *Atlantic*, November 3. https://www.theatlantic.com/entertainment/archive/2011/11/the-never-ending-debate-over-women-in-metal-and-hard-rock/247795/.

———. 2014. "Fighting Violence Against Women in India with Heavy Metal." *Atlantic*, March 10. https://www.theatlantic.com/entertainment/archive/2014/03/fighting-violence-against-women-in-india-with-heavy-metal/283963/.

———. 2018. "With #KillTheKing, Heavy Metal Is Having Its #MeToo Moment." Vice, March 19. https://www.vice.com/en_asia/article/9kg9ez/with-killtheking-heavy-metal-is-having-its-metoo-moment.

———. 2019. "Ten Divine, Diabolical Feminine Artists Challenging Heavy Metal Machismo." Bandcamp, September 18. https://daily.bandcamp.com/lists/feminine-expression-in-metal-guide.

Kitteringham, Sarah. 2014. *Extreme Conditions Demand Extreme Responses: The Treatment of Women in Black Metal, Death Metal, Doom Metal, and Grindcore*. Unpublished master's thesis, University of Calgary. http://hdl.handle.net/11023/1293.

Kores, Maiken A. 2020. "Girls, Girls, Girls—Women in Glam Metal." Pp. 92–118 in *Words, Music and Gender*, edited by Michelle Gadpaille and Victor Kennedy. Newcastle Upon Tyne, UK: Cambridge Scholars.

Kramer, Karen Z., Erin L. Kelly, and Jan B. McColloch. 2015. "Stay-at-Home Fathers: Definition and Characteristics Based on 34 Years of CPS Data." *Journal of Family Issues* 36(12): 1651–73.

Krenske, Leigh, and Jim McKay. 2000. "'Hard and Heavy': Gender and Power in a Heavy Metal Music Subculture." *Gender, Place, and Culture: A Journal of Feminist Geography* 7(3): 287–304.

Kummer, Jenna. 2016a. *"Lipstick and Leather": Recontextualizations of Glam Metal's Style and Signification.* MA thesis, University of Lethbridge. https://opus.uleth.ca/handle/10133/4490.

———. 2016b. "Powerslaves? Navigating Femininity in Heavy Metal." Pp. 145–66 in *Heavy Metal Studies and Popular Culture*, edited by Brenda Gardenour Walter, Gabby Riches, Dave Snell, and Bryan Bardine. Basingstoke, UK: Palgrave Macmillan.

———. 2017. "'I Remember You': Exploring Glam Metal's Re-Emergence in Contemporary Metal Music Markets." *Metal Music Studies* 3(3): 421–36.

Laaksonen, Laura, Antti Ainamo, and Toni-Matti Karjalainen. 2011. "Entrepreneurial Passion: An Explorative Case Study of Four Metal Music Ventures." *Journal of Research in Marketing and Entrepreneurship* 13(1): 18–36.

Lapolla, Lex. 2016. "The Problem with 'Female Fronted Metal'." Odyssey, October 24. https://www.theodysseyonline.com/problem-with-female-fronted-metal.

Larsson, Susanna. 2013. "'I Bang My Head, Therefore I Am': Constructing Individual and Social Authenticity in the Heavy Metal Subculture." *Young* 21(1): 95–110.

Lawless, Jennifer L. 2004. "Politics of Presence? Congresswomen and Symbolic Representation." *Political Research Quarterly* 57: 81–99.

Leigh, Amari Rose. 2019. "For Indonesia's All-Girl Heavy Metal Band, Music Is the 'Voice of Resistance.'" Malala, December 4. https://assembly.malala.org/stories/voice-of-baceprot-challenging-stereotypes.

LeVine, Mark. 2008. "Heavy Metal Muslims: The Rise of a Post-Islamist Public Sphere." *Contemporary Islam* 2(3): 229–49.

Lind, Joshua H. 2013. "The Ghost-Father in 1980s Heavy Metal." *Journal of the Fantastic in the Arts* 24(2): 275–88.

Lindner, Danielle, Stacey Tantleff-Dunn, and Florian Jentsch. 2012. "Social Comparison and the 'Circle of Objectification.'" *Sex Roles* 67: 222–35.

Litchfield, Chelsea, Emma Kavanagh, Jaquelyn Osborne, and Ian Jones. 2018. "Social Media and the Politics of Gender, Race, and Identity: The Case of Serena Williams." *European Journal for Sport and Society* 15(2): 154–70.

Lipman-Blumen, Jean. 1976. "Toward a Homosocial Theory of Sex Roles: An Explanation of the Sex Segregation of Social Institutions." *Signs* 1(3): 15–31.

Lorber, Judith, and Patricia Yancey Martin. 2007. "The Socially Constructed Body: Insights from Feminist Theory." Pp. 226–48 in *Illuminating Social Life: Classic and Contemporary Theory Revisited*, 4th edition, edited by Peter Kivisto. Thousand Oaks, CA: Pine Forge Press.

Lovelock, Michael. 2019. "Gay and Happy: (Proto-)Homonormativity, Emotion and Popular Culture." *Sexualities* 22(4): 549–65.

Lowles, Genevieve. 2018. "Woman in the Pit: How I Found Power and Safety at Heavy Metal Concerts." The Refresh, May 15. http://www.therefresh.co/2018/05/15/woman-in-the-pit-how-i-found-power-and-safety-at-heavy-metal-concerts/.

Loye, Kristy. 2015. "Metal's Problem with Women Is Not Going Away Anytime Soon." Houston Press, November 11. https://www.houstonpress.com/music/metals-problem-with-women-is-not-going-away-anytime-soon-7858411.

Lumsden, Karen. 2010. "Gendered Performances in a Male-Dominated Subculture: 'Girl Racers', Car Modification, and the Quest for Masculinity." *Sociological Research Online* 15(3): 6–17.

Luyten, Tom. 2016. "On the Phenomenon of 'Crowd Killing.'" Medium, March 13. https://medium.com/@tomluyten/on-the-phenomenon-of-crowd-killing-564364aa8f75.

Madoo Lengermann, Patricia, and Gillian Niebrugge. 1998. *The Women Founders: Sociology and Social Theory, 1830–1930.* Long Grove, IL: Waveland Press.

Magnotta, Andrew. 2017. "Bruce Dickinson Isn't Bothered by Posers Wearing Iron Maiden Shirts." iHeart Radio, November 7. https://www.iheart.com/content/2017-11-07-bruce-dickinson-isnt-bothered-by-posers-wearing-iron-maiden-shirts/.

Merton, Robert K. 1972. "Insiders and Outsiders: A Chapter in the Sociology of Knowledge." *American Journal of Sociology* 77: 9–47.

Merton, Robert K. 1995. "The Thomas Theorem and the Matthew Effect." *Social Forces* 74(2): 379–422.

Messerschmidt, James W. 2009. "Doing Gender: The Impact and Future of a Salient Sociological Concept." *Gender and Society* 23(1): 85–88.

Messner, Michael A., Margaret Carlisle Duncan, and Kerry Jensen. 1993. "Separating the Men from the Girls: The Gendered Language of Televised Sports." *Gender and Society* 7(1): 121–37.

Miller, Diana L. 2014. "Symbolic Capital and Gender: Evidence from Two Cultural Fields." *Cultural Sociology* 8(4): 462–82.

———. 2016. "Gender, Field, and Habitus: How Gendered Dispositions Reproduce Fields of Cultural Production." *Sociological Forum* 31(2): 330–53.

———. 2017. "Gender and Performance Capital among Local Musicians." *Qualitative Sociology* 40(3): 263–86.

Miller, Jody. 1998. "Gender and Victimization Risk among Young Women in Gangs." *Journal of Research in Crime and Delinquency* 35(4): 429–53.

———. 2001. *One of the Guys: Girls, Gangs and Gender.* New York: Oxford University Press.

———. 2002. "The Strengths and Limits of 'Doing Gender' for Understanding Street Crime." *Theoretical Criminology* 6(4): 433–60.

Mombelet, Alexis. 2005. "La Musique Metal: Des 'Éclats de Religion' et une Liturgie. Pour une Compréhension Sociologique des Concerts de Metal Comme Rites Contemporains." *Sociétés* 2: 25–51.

Morgan, Laurie A., and Karin A. Martin. 2006. "Taking Women Professionals Out of the Office: The Case of Women in Sales." *Gender and Society* 20(1): 108–28.

Morris, Martin. 2014. "Negative Dialectics in Music: Adorno and Heavy Metal." *European Journal of Cultural Studies* 17(5): 549–66.

———. 2015. "Extreme Heavy Metal Music and Critical Theory." *Germanic Review: Literature, Culture, Theory* 90(4): 285–303.

Moynihan, Michael, and Didrik Søderlind. 2003. *Lords of Chaos: The Bloody Rise of the Satanic Metal Underground.* Revised and expanded edition. Los Angeles, CA: Feral House.

Mulvey, Laura. 1975. "Visual Pleasure and Narrative Cinema." *Screen* 16(3): 6–18.

Murnen, Sarah, Greenfield, Abigail Younger, and Hope Boyd. 2016. "Boys Act and Girls Appear: A Content Analysis of Gender Stereotypes Associated with Characters in Children's Popular Culture." *Sex Roles* 74(1–2): 78–91.

Newheiser, Anna-Kaisa, Marianne LaFrance, and John F. Dovidio. 2010. "Others as Objects: How Women and Men Perceive the Consequences of Self-Objectification." *Sex Roles* 63: 657–71.

Nicholson, Linda. 1994. "Interpreting Gender." *Signs* 20(1): 79–105.

Nordström, Susanna, and Marcus Herz. 2013. "'It's a Matter of Eating or Being Eaten': Gender Positioning and Difference Making in the Heavy Metal Subculture." *European Journal of Cultural Studies* 16(4): 453–67.

O'Hagan, Lauren. 2021a. "The Anatomy of a Battle Jacket: A Multimodal Ethnographic Perspective." *Journal of Contemporary Ethnography* 50(2): 147–75.

———. 2021b. "'My Musical Armor': Exploring Metalhead Identity through the Battle Jacket." *Rock Music Studies*, February 2. https://doi.org/10.1080/19401159.2021.1872763.

Overell, Rosemary. 2012. "'[I] Hate Girls and Emo[tion]s': Negotiating Masculinity in Grindcore Music." *Popular Music History* 6(1): 198–223.

———. 2014. *Affective Intensities in Extreme Music Scenes: Cases from Australia and Japan.* Basingstoke, UK: Palgrave Macmillan.

Palmer, Craig T. 2005. "Mummers and Moshers: Two Rituals of Trust in Changing Social Environments." *Ethnology* 44(2): 147–66.

Pasbani, Robert. 2017. "Dee Snider Calls Out Celebrities Wearing Metal Shirts: 'Metal Is Not Ironic. Dicks.'" Metal Injection, October 18. https://metalinjection.net/news/dee-snider-calls-out-celebrities-wearing-metal-shirts-metal-is-not-ironic-dicks.

———. 2019. "Couple Filmed Engaging in Oral Sex during Behemoth Show." Metal Injection, July 7. https://metalinjection.net/news/yes/couple-filmed-engaging-in-oral-sex-during-behemoth-show.

———. 2020. "Major Booking Agent Accused of Sexual Harassment, Shady Business Practices." Metal Injection, September 28. https://metalinjection.net/shocking-revelations/major-booking-agent-accused-of-sexual-harassment-shady-business-practices.

Patterson, Jamie E. 2016a. "'Getting My Soul Back': Empowerment Narratives and Identities among Women in Extreme Metal in North Carolina." Pp. 245–60 in *Global Metal Music and Culture Studies: Current Directions in Metal Studies*, edited by Andy R. Brown, Karl Spracklen, Keith Kahn-Harris, and Niall W. R. Scott. New York: Routledge.

———. 2016b. "Blasting Britney on the Way to Goatwhore: Identity and Authenticity among Female-Identified Fans in Semi-Rural North Carolina." Pp. 123–44 in *Heavy Metal Studies and Popular Culture*, edited by Brenda Gardenour Walter, Gabby Riches, Dave Snell, and Bryan Bardine, Basingstoke, UK: Palgrave Macmillan.

Pilgeram, Ryanne. 2007. "'Ass-kicking' Women: Doing and Undoing Gender in a US Livestock Auction." *Gender, Work, and Organization* 14(6): 572–95.

Platt, Lucinda, and Javier Polavieja. 2016. "Saying and Doing Gender: Intergenerational Transmission of Attitudes towards the Sexual Division of Labour." *European Sociological Review* 32(6): 820–34.

Porrovecchio, Mark J. 2017. "Female Rhetoric: Identity, Persona and the Academic and Popular Divide in the (Cultural and Critical) Study of Metal." *Metal Music Studies* 3(2): 329–34.

Purcell, Natalie J. 2015. *Death Metal Music: The Passion and Politics of a Subculture.* Jefferson, NC: McFarland.

Rademacher, Heidi E. 2015. "'Men of Iron Will': Idealized Gender in Christian Heavy Metal." *Social Compass* 62(4): 632–48.

Rafalovich, Adam. 2006. "Broken and Becoming God-Sized: Contemporary Metal Music and Masculine Individualism." *Symbolic Interaction* 29(1): 19–32.

Ramon, Shulamit, Michele Lloyd, and Bridget Penhale (eds.). 2021. *Gendered Domestic Violence and Abuse in Popular Culture*. Bingley, UK: Emerald.

Random Name Generator. http://random-name-generator.info/.

Recours, Robin, François Aussaguel, and Nick Trujillo. 2009. "Metal Music and Mental Health in France." *Culture, Medicine & Psychiatry* 33(3): 473–88.

Riches, Gabby. 2015. "Re-Conceptualizing Women's Marginalization in Heavy Metal: A Feminist Post-Structuralist Perspective." *Metal Music Studies* 1(2): 263–70.

Riches, Gabrielle. 2011. "Embracing the Chaos: Mosh Pits, Extreme Metal Music and Liminality." *Journal for Cultural Research* 15(3): 315–32.

———. 2012. *"Caught in a Mosh": Moshpit Culture, Extreme Metal Music, and the Reconceptualization of Leisure*. MA thesis, University of Alberta.

———. 2014. "Brothers of Metal! Heavy Metal Masculinities, Moshpit Practices and Homosociality." Pp. 88–105 in *Debating Modern Masculinities: Change, Continuity, Crisis?*, edited by S. Roberts. London: Palgrave Pivot.

Riches, Gabrielle, Brett Lashua, and Karl Spracklen. 2013. "Female, Mosher, Transgressor: A 'Moshography' of Transgressive Practices within the Leeds Extreme Metal Scene." *IASPM@Journal* 4(1). https://iaspmjournal.net/index.php/IASPM_Journal/article/view/652/0.

Ritlop, Tina. 2020. "'You Scream Like a Girl': Growling and Screaming Female Voices in Metal Music." Pp. 149–57 in *Words, Music and Gender*, edited by Michelle Gadpaille and Victor Kennedy. Newcastle Upon Tyne, UK: Cambridge Scholars.

Rival, Laura, Don Slater, and Daniel Miller. 1998. "Sex and Sociality: Comparative Ethnographies of Sexual Objectification." *Theory, Culture & Society* 15(3–4): 295–321.

Roberts, Tomi-Ann, and Jennifer Y. Gettman. 2004. "Mere Exposure: Gender Differences in the Negative Effects of Priming a State of Self-Objectification." *Sex Roles* 51: 17–27.

Rogers, Anna S. 2015. *Women in Hypermasculine Environments: An Analysis of Gender Dynamics in the Heavy Metal Subculture*. MA thesis, University of South Carolina. https://scholarcommons.sc.edu/etd/3155/.

———. 2019. "Are Disney Characters 'Frozen' in Stereotypes? An Intersectional Analysis of *Frozen*." *Education Sciences & Society* 10(2): 23–41.

Rosen, Leora N., Kathryn H. Knudson, and Peggy Fancher. 2003. "Cohesion and the Culture of Hypermasculinity in U.S. Army Units." *Armed Forces & Society* 29(3): 325–51.

Rosenblatt, Josh. 2017. "Metal Singer Calls Out Groper at Rock Festival." Newser, August 20. https://www.newser.com/story/247444/heavy-metal-singer-stops-sexual-assault-at-show.html.

Rubin, Alan, Daniel West, and Wendy Mitchell. 2001. "Differences in Aggression, Attitudes toward Women, and Distrust as Reflected in Popular Music Preferences." *Media Psychology* 3(1): 25–42.

Savigny, Heather, and Julian Schaap. 2018. "Putting the 'Studies' Back in Metal Music Studies." *Metal Music Studies* 4(3): 549–57.

Savigny, Heather, and Sam Sleight. 2015. "Postfeminism and Heavy Metal in the United Kingdom: Sexy or Sexist?," *Metal Music Studies* 1(3): 341–57.

Schaap, Julian, and Pauwke Berkers. 2014. "Grunting Alone? Online Gender Inequality in Extreme Metal Music." *IASPM@Journal* 4(1). http://www.iaspmjournal.net/index.php/IASPM_Journal/article/view/675/pdf.

Schiller, Rebecca. 2012. "Isn't It Time We Stopped Blaming Violent Behaviour on Heavy Metal?" NME Blog, January 9. https://www.nme.com/blogs/nme-blogs/isnt-it-time-we-stopped-blaming-violent-behaviour-on-heavy-metal-780766#XZYPEXbjmrAjOc7I.99.

Schippers, Mimi. 2000. "The Social Organization of Sexuality and Gender in Alternative Hard Rock: An Analysis of Intersectionality." *Gender and Society* 14(6): 747–64.

Scott, Niall. 2016. "The Monstrous Male and Myths of Masculinity in Heavy Metal." Pp. 121–32 in *Heavy Metal, Gender and Sexuality: Interdisciplinary Approaches*, edited by Florian Heesch and Niall Scott. Abingdon, UK: Routledge.

Shadrack, Jasmine H. 2017. "From Enslavement to Obliteration: Extreme Metal's Problem with Women." Pp. 170–84 in *Under My Thumb: Songs That Hate Women and the Women Who Love Them*, edited by Rhian E. Jones and Elie Davies. London: Repeater.

———. 2018. "Mater Omnium and the Cosmic Womb of the Abyss: Nomadic Interiorities and Matrifocal Black Metal Performance." *Metal Music Studies* 4(2): 281–92.

———. 2021. *Black Metal, Trauma, Subjectivity and Sound: Screaming the Abyss.* Bingley, UK: Emerald.

Shiakallis, Paul. 2015. "The Leather-Clad Rock Queens of Botswana." *Guardian*, December 25. https://www.theguardian.com/world/gallery/2015/dec/25/the-leather-clad-rock-queens-of-botswana-in-pictures.

Simmel, Georg. (1908) 1971. "The Stranger." Pp. 143–50 in *On Individuality and Social Forms*, edited by Donald N. Levine. Chicago: University of Chicago Press.

Singleton, Royce A., Jr., and Bruce C. Straits. 2010. *Approaches to Social Research.* 5th edition. New York: Oxford University Press.

Sisjord, Mari Kristin, and Elsa Kristiansen. 2009. "Elite Women Wrestlers' Muscles: Physical Strength and a Social Burden." *International Review for the Sociology of Sport* 44: 231–46.

Sloat, Lisa J. 1998. "Incubus: Male Songwriters' Portrayal of Women's Sexuality in Pop Metal Music." Pp. 286–301 in *Youth Culture: Identity in a Postmodern World*, edited by Jonathon S. Epstein. Malden, MA: Blackwell.

Snell, Dave, and Darrin Hodgetts. 2007. "Heavy Metal, Identity and the Social Negotiation of a Community of Practice." *Journal of Community & Applied Social Psychology* 17(6): 430–45.

Sollee, Kristen. 2015. "Mining the Motherload: Mastodon's #twerkgate and Sexual Objectification in Metal." *Metal Music Studies* 1(2): 271–77.

Solomon, Rosie. 2021. "Out of the Closet and into the Pit: The Queer Artists Revolutionising Extreme Metal." *Metal Hammer*, March 11. https://www.loudersound.com/features/out-of-the-closet-and-into-the-pit-the-queer-artists-revolutionising-extreme-metal.

Spracklen, Karl. 2013. "Nazi Punks Folk Off: Leisure, Nationalism, Cultural Identity and the Consumption of Metal and Folk Music." *Leisure Studies* 32(4): 415–28.

Spracklen, Karl, Andy R. Brown, and Keith Kahn-Harris. 2011. "Introduction: Metal Studies? Cultural Research in the Heavy Metal Scene." *Journal for Cultural Research* 15(3): 209–12.

Stack, Steven, Jim Gundlach, and Jimmie L. Reeves. 1994. "The Heavy Metal Subculture and Suicide." *Suicide and Life-Threatening Behavior* 24(1): 15–23.

St. Lawrence, Janet S., and Doris J. Joyner. 1991. "The Effects of Sexually Violent Rock Music on Males' Acceptance of Violence Against Women." *Psychology of Women Quarterly* 15(1): 49–63.

Stitched Up Heart. 2018. Instagram post, March 3. https://www.instagram.com/p/Bf3_9NdFPoM/.

Swami, Viren, Fiona Malpass, David Havard, Karis Benford, Ana Costescu, Angeliki Sofitiki, and Donna Taylor. 2013. "Metalheads: The Influence of Personality and Individual Differences on Preference for Heavy Metal." *Psychology of Aesthetics, Creativity & the Arts* 7(4): 377–83.

Theberge, Nancy. 1993. "The Construction of Gender in Sport: Women, Coaching, and the Naturalization of Difference." *Social Problems* 40(3): 301–13.

Thorpe, Holly. 2010. "Bourdieu, Gender Reflexivity, and Physical Culture: A Case of Masculinities in the Snowboarding Field." *Journal of Sport and Social Issues* 34: 176–214.

Torreiro, Gustavo. 2020. "Heavy Metal as a Subculture in Argentina: Identity and Resistance." Pp. 2–15 in *Heavy Metal Music in Argentina: In Black We Are Seen*, edited by Emiliano Scaricaciottoli, Nelson Varas-Díaz, and Daniel Nevárez Araujo. Bristol, UK: Intellect.

Townsend, Caroline. 2020. "For Girls Who Want to Rock (We Exclude You): Experiences of Discrimination in Indonesian Alternative Music Scenes." *Intersections: Gender & Sexuality in Asia & the Pacific* (44): 1–17.

Trier-Bieniek, Adrienne. 2013. *Sing Us a Song, Piano Woman: Female Fans and the Music of Tori Amos*. Metuchen, NJ: Scarecrow Press.

Turbé, Sophie. 2016. "Puissance, Force et Musique Metal: Quand les Filles s'Approprient les Codes de la Masculinité." *Ethnologie Française* 46(1): 93–102.

Vanhorn, Teri. 1999. "Two Woodstock Fans Allegedly Raped in Mosh Pits." MTV, July 30. http://www.mtv.com/news/516319/two-woodstock-fans-allegedly-raped-in-mosh-pits/.

Varas-Díaz, Nelson. 2019. "Songs of Injustice: Heavy Metal in Latin America (Full Movie)." YouTube video, posted on April 8. https://www.youtube.com/watch?v=Yb4u3Q1APHk.

Varas-Díaz, Nelson, Daniel Nevárez Araújo, and Eliut Rivera-Segarra (eds.). 2021. *Heavy Metal Music in Latin America: Perspectives from the Distorted South*. Lanham, MD: Lexington Books.

Vasan, Sonia. 2010. "'Den Mothers' and 'Band Whores': Gender, Sex and Power in the Death Metal Scene." Pp. 67–77 in *Heavy Fundamentalisms: Music, Metal and Politics*, edited by R. Hill and K. Spracklen. Leiden, The Netherlands: Brill.

———. 2011. "The Price of Rebellion: Gender Boundaries in the Death Metal Scene." *Journal for Cultural Research* 15(3): 333–49.

———. 2016. "Gender and Power in the Death Metal Scene: A Social Exchange Perspective." Pp. 261–76 in *Global Metal Music and Culture Studies: Current Directions in Metal Studies*, edited by Andy R. Brown, Karl Spracklen, Keith Kahn-Harris, and Niall W. R. Scott. New York: Routledge.

Verden, Paul, Kathleen Dunleavy, and Charles H. Powers. 1989. "Heavy Metal Mania and Adolescent Delinquency." *Popular Music and Society* 13(1): 73–82.

Vincent, John, Paul M. Pedersen, Warren A. Whisenant, and Dwayne Massey. 2007. "Analysing the Print Media Coverage of Professional Tennis Players: British Newspaper Narratives about Female Competitors in the Wimbledon Championships." *International Journal of Sport Management and Marketing* 2(3): 281–300.

Walser, Robert. 1993. *Running with the Devil: Power, Gender, and Madness in Heavy Metal Music.* Middletown, CT: Wesleyan University Press.

Weber, Max. (1949) 2011. *Methodology of Social Sciences.* New Brunswick, NJ: Transaction.

Weinstein, Deena. 1991. *Heavy Metal: A Cultural Sociology.* New York: Lexington Books.

———. 2000. *Heavy Metal: The Music and Its Culture.* Revised edition. Boston: Da Capo Press.

———. 2009. "The Empowering Masculinity of British Heavy Metal." Pp. 17–32 in *Heavy Metal Music in Britain,* edited by In Gerd Bayer. Burlington, VT: Ashgate.

———. 2016. "Playing with Gender in the Key of Metal." Pp. 11–25 in *Heavy Metal, Gender and Sexuality: Interdisciplinary Approaches,* edited by Florian Heesch and Niall Scott. Abingdon, UK: Routledge.

Wensing, Emma H., and Toni Bruce. 2003. "Bending the Rules: Media Representations of Gender During an International Sporting Event." *International Review for the Sociology of Sport* 38(4): 387–96.

West, Candace, and Sarah Fenstermaker. 1995. "Doing Difference." *Gender and Society* 9(1): 8–37.

West, Candace, and Don H. Zimmerman. 1987. "Doing Gender." *Gender & Society* 1(2): 125–51.

———. 2009. "Accounting for Doing Gender." *Gender and Society* 23(1): 112–22.

Westmarland, Nicole. 2001. "The Quantitative/Qualitative Debate and Feminist Research: A Subjective View of Objectivity." *Forum: Qualitative Social Research* 2(1), article 13. http://nbn-resolving.de/urn:nbn:de:0114-fqs0101135.

Whiteley, Shelia. 2000. *Women and Popular Music: Sexuality, Identity and Subjectivity.* Oxford, UK: Routledge.

Wickes, Rebecca, and Michael Emmison. 2007. "They Are All 'Doing Gender' but Are They All Passing? A Case Study of the Appropriation of a Sociological Concept." *Sociological Review* 55(2): 311–30.

Wikipedia. n.d. "Heavy Metal Music." Accessed February 8, 2021. https://en.wikipedia.org/wiki/Heavy_metal_music.

Wildberger, Jared, and Ingrid G. Farreras. 2016. "Helping Behavior in Heavy Metal Concerts." *Modern Psychological Studies* 22(1): 97–103.

Wolkomir, Michelle. 2012. "'You Fold Like a Little Girl': (Hetero)Gender Framing and Competitive Strategies of Men and Women in No Limit Texas Hold 'Em Poker Games." *Qualitative Sociology* 35: 407–26.

Wong, Cynthia P. 2011. "'A Dream Return to Tang Dynasty': Masculinity, Male Camaraderie, and Chinese Heavy Metal in the 1990s." Pp. 63–85 in *Metal Rules the Globe: Heavy Metal Music Around the World,* edited by Jeremy Wallach, Harris Berger, and Paul Greene. Durham, NC: Duke University Press.

Wright, Laura. 2015. "Transcending the Form, Advancing the Norm: Queer-Post Structrualism in Post-Metal." Pp. 247–56 in *Modern Heavy Metal: Markets, Practices and Cultures,* edited by T. Karjalainen and K. Kärki. Helsinki: Aalto University.

Yang, Qinghua, and Cong Li. 2014. "Mozart or Metallica, Who Makes You More Attractive? A Mediated Moderation Test of Music, Gender, Personality, and Attractiveness in Cyberspace." *Computers in Human Behavior* 29(6): 2796–804.

Young, Amy M., Michele Morales, Sean Esteban Mccabe, Carol J. Boyd and Hannah D'arcy. 2005. "Drinking Like a Guy: Frequent Binge Drinking among Undergraduate Women." *Substance Use & Misuse* 40(2): 241–67.

INDEX

CPSIA information can be obtained
at www.ICGtesting.com
Printed in the USA
LVHW090730081021
699883LV00001B/47